Table of Con...

©www.CoreCommonStandards.com

K

Common Core State Standards

Kindergarten Workbook
TEACHER EDITION

Grade K
- **Math Standards**
- **English Standards**

Worksheets that teach every
Common Core Standard!

Name: _____

Camping

Directions: Read, or listen to the teacher read, the passage below about camping. Answer the questions about the text. Ask your own question that can be answered by reading the text.

Camping is fun. We camp in a tent and cook on a campfire. We roast marshmallows and sing songs, too. My dad takes us fishing on the lake, and mom pushes us on the swings. My favorite camping food is hot dogs that we cook on long sticks over the fire. At night we catch fireflies and then let them go. We sleep in sleeping bags and listen to the crickets chirp.
I love camping!

Answer these questions about the text.

1. Does the boy like camping?

_____

Yes. He loves camping.

2. What is his favorite camping food?

_____

His favorite food is hot dogs.

3. Who fishes with the boy?

_____

Dad fishes with the boy.

Ask a question about this text.

_____

Answers will vary.

_____

_____

Standard: Reading I Literature I RL.K.1

Name: _____

Puckles

Directions: Read, or listen to the teacher read, the passage below about Puckles. Answer the questions about the text. Ask your own question that can be answered by reading the text.

Mom surprised us today with a new dog! He is a beagle and is white with brown spots and long, floppy ears. We named our new dog Puckles. Puckles likes to jump and run, but he falls over a lot which makes me smile. Puckles did something funny when he ate. He picked up one little piece of food, walked over to the couch, sat down, and ate the piece. Then he walked back over for one more. Puckles will be fun to have as a pet. Thanks mom!

Answer these questions about the text.

1. What does Puckles look like?

Puckles is white and brown. He has long, floppy ears.

2. Why did the girl smile?

Puckles falls down and makes her smile.

3. Who brought Puckles home?

Mom brought Puckles home.

Ask a question about this text.

questions and answers vary

Reading: Literature

Story Details

Think about the details in the story. Use this organizer to write key details about the text.

detail

detail

detail

detail

detail

Title of Story

answers vary

Common Core Standard: RL.K.1

Reading: Literature

Story Details

Think about the story you just read. Write the key details from the story in the boxes below.

answers vary

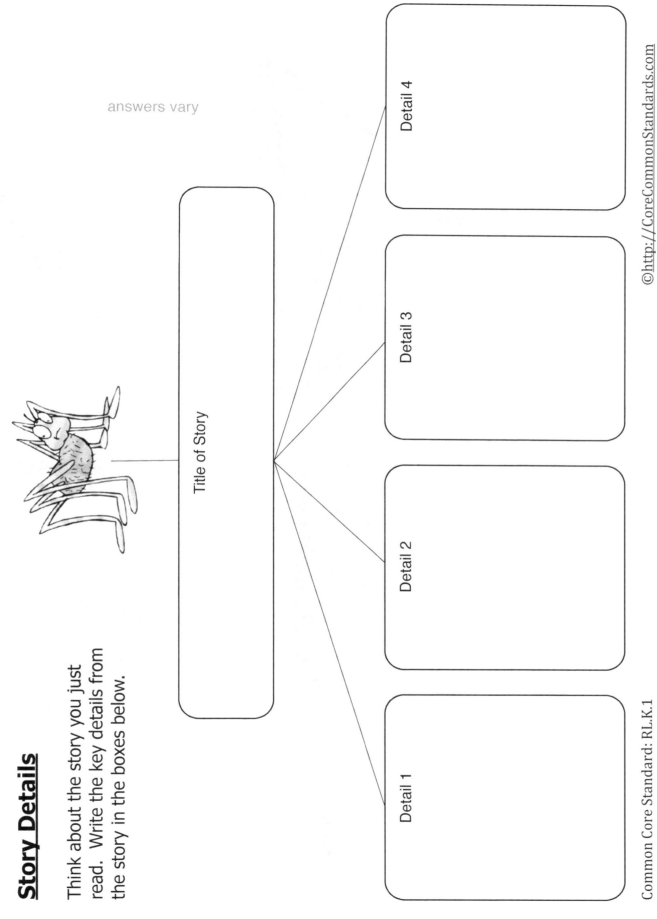

Title of Story

Detail 1

Detail 2

Detail 3

Detail 4

Common Core Standard: RL.K.1

Level: Kindergarten   Name: _____

Retelling a Story

Directions: Listen to the teacher read a story to you.   Draw and write about the most important parts at the beginning, middle, and end of the story.

Beginning

_____

- -

answers vary

_____

Middle

_____

- -

answers vary

_____

_____

- -

_____

End

_____

- -

answers vary

_____

Name: _____

The Three Little Pigs

Directions: Read, or listen to the teacher read, *The Three Little Pigs.* Retell the story.

The Three Little Pigs

Once upon a time there were three little pigs. One pig built a house of straw. One pig built his house with sticks. They built their houses very quickly, then played all because they were lazy. The third little pig worked hard all day and built his house with bricks.

A big bad wolf saw the two little pigs while they played and thought, "What a yummy dinner they will make!" Later that night, the big bad wolf went to the first house and huffed and puffed and blew the house down in minutes. The scared little pig ran to the second pig's house that was made of sticks. The big bad wolf went to his house and huffed and puffed and blew the house down right away. Now, the two little pigs were really scared and ran to the third pig's house that was made of bricks.

The big bad wolf tried to huff and puff and blow the house down, but he could not. He kept trying for hours but the house was very strong and the little pigs were safe inside. The wolf decided to go down the chimney, but the third little pig boiled a big pot of water and put it in the fireplace. The wolf fell into it and died.

The two little pigs felt bad for having been so lazy. The third pig helped them build their houses out of brick, and the three pigs lived happily ever after.

Beginning
Answers may vary, but there should be a definite distinction between the beginning, middle, and end.
pigs build houses

Middle
the wolf attacks, blows down two houses

End
the wolf can't blow down last house, tries, dies, and lessons are learned

Reading: Literature

Retell The Story

1. Read The Itsy Bitsy Spider.
2. Fill in the details of the story below.
3. Retell the story using the details.

Name: _____

answers vary

Title of Story

The Itsy Bitsy Spider

Detail 4

Detail 3

Detail 2

Detail 1

Common Core Standard: RL.K.2

Level: Kindergarten   Name: _____

Tell About the Story

Directions: Read, or listen to the teacher read, a story you know. Retell the story by filling in the parrot's speech bubbles.

answers vary
_____
Book Title

Who Are the Main Characters?

Where Does the Story Take Place?

What's the Problem

How Was it Solved?

Name: _____

Important Parts of the Story

Directions: Read, or listen to the teacher read, a story. Draw a picture and write important words about the characters, setting, and events from the story.

answers vary
_____
Book Title

Who Are the Main Characters?

Where Does the Story Take Place?

Important Event

Reading: Literature

Name: _____

Characters, Settings and Events

With prompting and support, identify characters, settings, and major events in a story.

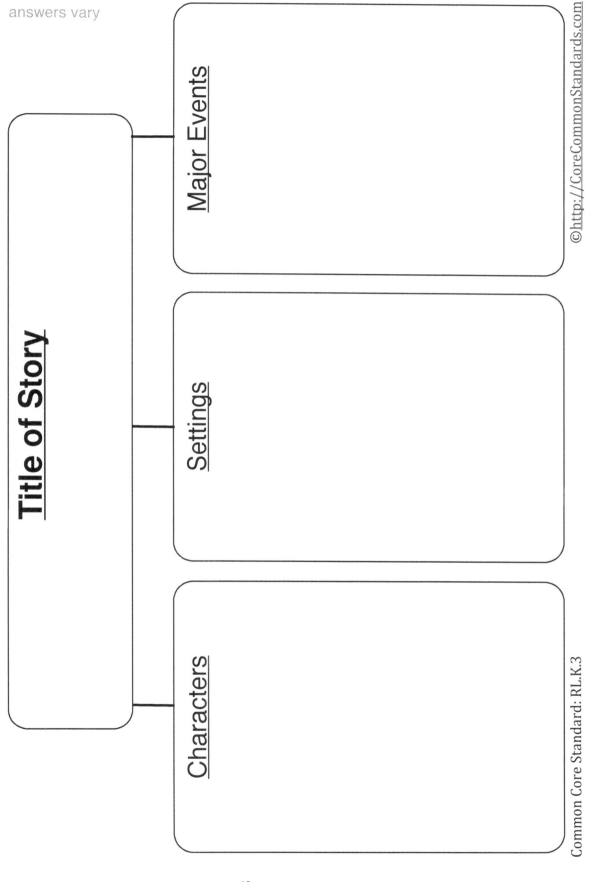

Title of Story

Major Events

Settings

Characters

©http://CoreCommonStandards.com

Common Core Standard: RL.K.3

13

Name: _____

What's That Word?

Directions: Read the passages below. Figure out the meaning of each underlined word by listening to the clues in each passage, looking at the picture, and thinking about what's happening.

When Tommy saw the fish at the end of his line, he cheered and smiled because he was so <u>elated.</u>

What do you think the word <u>elated</u> means?

_____

happy, because he cheered and smiled.

_____

_____

Sandra was upset when she saw that she had <u>damaged</u> mom's new vase.

What do you think the word <u>damaged</u> means?

_____

broken, because of the broken vase in the picture.

_____

_____

Kitty had a lot of <u>discomfort</u> when goldfish bit him in the tail.

What do you think the word <u>discomfort</u> means?

_____

hurt, because the cat got bitten by the goldfish.

_____

_____

Slinky was <u>terrified</u> when he went down on the fast ride.

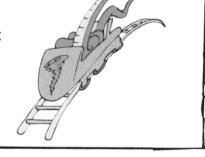

What do you think the word <u>terrified</u> means?

_____

scared, because he does not look happy on the ride.

_____

_____

Standard: Reading I Literature I RL.K.4

Name: _____

Football

Directions: Read, or listen to the teacher read, the passage below about football. Write any unknown words in the box. Talk about the words you do not know with a partner or your teacher.

Rob and Sam like to play football. Mr. Cooper says football is good exercise. Dad says football makes you tough.   Big brother says it gets you into college. Mom says it can get you into a hospital. Rob and Sam just like it because it is a fun activity. So, they challenge each other every day.

Do you see any words that you do not know?

Write them in the space below.

Answers vary. Sample words might be: college, tough, exercise, challenge, activity, hospital...

Now try to answer these questions:

Think about what is happening in the story.   What do you think the word means?

What clues can help you?

What does the word look like?

Level: Kindergarten

Name: _____

Do I Know These Words?

Read a story. Use the organizer below to list words from the story. Ask and answer questions about unknown words in the text.

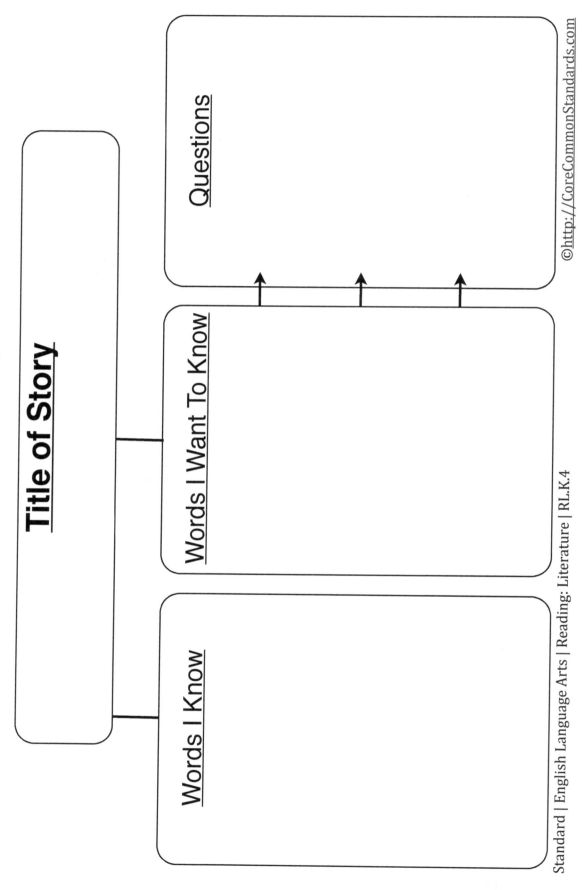

Title of Story

Words I Know

Words I Want To Know

Questions

Standard | English Language Arts | Reading: Literature | RL.K.4

©http://CoreCommonStandards.com

Name: _____

What Kind of Story?

Directions: With your teacher's help, match the book cover to the type of story it is. (genre)

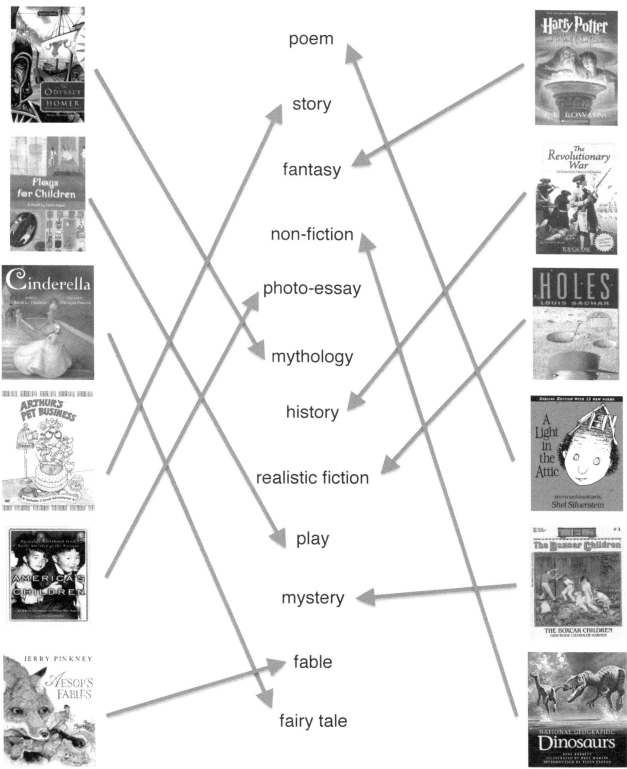

poem

story

fantasy

non-fiction

photo-essay

mythology

history

realistic fiction

play

mystery

fable

fairy tale

Standard: Reading I Literature I RL.K.5

©http://CoreCommonStandards.com

Name: _____

What I Am Reading

Directions: You are reading all kinds of stories. Write a title for each kind of book you read in Kindergarten throughout the year.

poem		date / /
story		date / /
fantasy		date / /
non-fiction		date / /
photo-essay		date / /
mythology		date / /
history		date / /
realistic fiction		date / /
play		date / /
mystery		date / /
fable		date / /
fairy tale		date / /

Standard: Reading I Literature I RL.K.5

©http://CoreCommonStandards.com

Level: Kindergarten

Name: _____

What Type of Story Is This?

Look through your collection of storybooks and poems.
Use the organizer below to sort out the different types of texts.

Poems
_____

Answers vary

Storybooks
_____

©http://CoreCommonStandards.com

Standard | English Language Arts | Reading: Literature | RL.K.5

Level: Kindergarten

Name: _____

What Type of Story Is This?

Look through your collection of books, magazines, and newspapers.
Use the organizer below to sort out the different types of texts that you found.

Books

Magazines

Newspapers

Answers Vary

Standard | English Language Arts | Reading: Literature | RL.K.5

Name: _____

Authors and Illustrators

Directions: Choose a story to read. Write the author's and illustrator's names. Write or explain how each person helps to tell the story.

The book I chose is

Answers vary
_____

Here is a picture from the book.

The author is _____

How does the author help to tell the story? (Is the author a character? Do you think the author made up the story or lived it? Does the author want us to learn something?)

The illustrator is _____

How does the illustrator help to tell the story? (Do the pictures drawn by the illustrator make you see the story better? Do the pictures help you understand the character better? Do they help you know where the story takes place?)

Standard: Reading I Literature I RL.K.6

©http://CoreCommonStandards.com

Level: Kindergarten   Name: _____

Authors and Illustrators : Amelia Bedelia

Directions: Read or listen to an Amelia Bedelia story. Write the author's and illustrator's names. Write or explain how each person helps to tell the story.

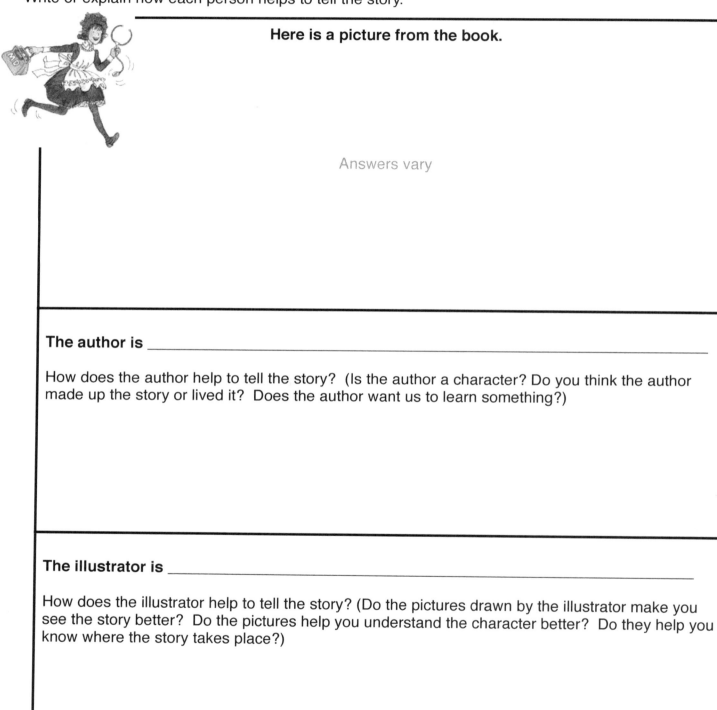

Here is a picture from the book.

Answers vary

The author is _____

How does the author help to tell the story? (Is the author a character? Do you think the author made up the story or lived it? Does the author want us to learn something?)

The illustrator is _____

How does the illustrator help to tell the story? (Do the pictures drawn by the illustrator make you see the story better? Do the pictures help you understand the character better? Do they help you know where the story takes place?)

Standard: Reading I Literature I RL.K.6   ©http://CoreCommonStandards.com

Author and Illustrator

Name the Title, Author, and Illustrator of a story.
Then, define the role of the author and the illustrator in telling the story.

Answers vary

Title of Story:

Author:

Illustrator:

How did the **author** help tell the story?

How did the **illustrator** help tell the story?

Standard | English Language Arts | Reading: Literature | RL.K.6

©http://CoreCommonStandards.com

Name: _____

Illustrations

Directions: Choose a story. Draw one illustration from the story. Think about why the illustrator drew that picture. Write or talk about how that illustration helps to tell the story.

The book I chose is

Answers vary

_____

Here is a picture from the book.

What can you tell about this illustration? How does it help to tell the story? When does this picture appear in the story?

_____
_____
_____
_____
_____
_____
_____
_____
_____
_____
_____

Standard: Reading I Literature I RL.K.7

©http://CoreCommonStandards.com

Name: _____

Illustrations

Directions: Look at the illustration from a story. Think about why the illustrator drew that picture. Write or talk about how that illustration helps to tell a story.

Here is a picture from a book.

What can you tell about this illustration? What do you notice?
How do you think it helps to tell the story?
Write what you think the picture is telling about the story.

Common answers are:
There are 6 mice.
There is a cat hiding or watching.
The mice look poor.
One mouse looks old, because he has a cane.
Most of the mice are young.
The mice are talking.

Level: Kindergarten   Name: _____

Comparing Characters

Directions: Choose two different characters from two different stories you have read. Think about something that happens to each character and how those events are the same, and how they are different.

Story 1:		Story 2:
_____	Answers Vary	_____
Author:		Author:
_____		_____

_____   _____
Character 1   Character 2

What is something that happens to this character in the story?	What is something that happens to this character in the story?

How are the characters' events the same?

How are the characters' events different?

Name: _____

Comparing Characters

Directions: Read, or listen to, two stories in which you would find each character. Think about something that happens to each character and how those events are the same, and how they are different.

Answers Vary

Charlie Brown	Arthur
What is something that happens to this character in the story?	What is something that happens to this character in the story?

How are the characters' events the same?

How are the characters' events different?

Standard: Reading I Literature I RL.K.9
Graphics(c)http://en.wikipedia.org   ©http://CoreCommonStandards.com

Level: Kindergarten   Name: _____

We Read Together

Directions: Use this form when you meet with a group and read a story.
Talk about the book. Share ideas.

Who is in my group?	**What book are we reading?**

Here are some of our thoughts.

Answers vary

Name: _____   READING LOG

What Are They Reading?

Directions: Keep track of the stories your students can read this year at grade level. Write the date each genre was read successfully.

Name	non-fiction story	realistic fiction story	fantasy story	informational story	poetry

Standard: Reading I Literature I RL.K.10

©http://CoreCommonStandards.com

Name: _____

Mammals

Directions: Read, or listen to the teacher read, the passage below about mammals. Answer the questions about the text. Ask your own question that can be answered by reading the text.

There are animals all around us. Many of the animals we see are mammals. Mammals are a group of animals that share the same characteristics. Mammals have fur, or hair. Mammal babies are born alive. Mammals do not lay eggs. Mammal mommies feed their babies milk. And mammals have lungs, so they breathe air. These animals are examples of mammals: dogs, cats, cows, pigs, sheep, lions, giraffes, mice, and even whales!

Answer these questions about the text.

1. What do mammals have on their bodies?

Mammals have fur or hair on their bodies.

2. How do mammals breathe?

Mammals breathe with lungs.

3. Name some mammals.

Some examples of mammals are: dogs, cats, cows, pigs, sheep, lions, giraffes, mice, and even whales!

Ask a question about this text.

Questions and answers will vary.

Name: _____

Pretzels

Directions: Read, or listen to the teacher read, the passage below about pretzels. Answer the questions about the text. Ask your own question that can be answered by reading the text.

Pretzels are a snack food that many people like. They are made from dough and can be soft or hard. Most pretzels are tied into a knot, but they can come in other shapes, too. Pretzels have salt on them and some people like to spread mustard on top. Pretzels can be as small as a quarter, or so big that you need two hands to eat it. Pretzels have been around for a long time.

Answer these questions about the text.

1. What are pretzels made from?

Pretzels are made from dough.

2. What size can pretzels be?

Pretzels can be small like a quarter or big enough that you need two hands to eat it. (They can be big or small.)

3. Are pretzels a new snack?

No, pretzels are not a new snack. Pretzels have been around for a long time.

Ask a question about this text.

Questions and answers will vary.

Standard: Reading l Informational Text l RI.K.1   ©http://CoreCommonStandards.com

Name: _____

<u>Senses</u>

Directions: Read, or listen to the teacher read, the passage below about the five senses. What is the main topic of the text? Use the web to write some details about the topic.

Humans have five senses. Seeing, hearing, smelling, touching, and tasting are our five senses. We use our senses to gather information about our world. We use our eyes to help us see. Our eyes have a lens like a camera. To smell things, we use our noses. Sounds we hear are heard with our ears. Our fingers, and the rest of our skin, allows us to feel things. And, we use our mouths, not just to talk, but to taste foods. Our five senses help us understand the world around us.

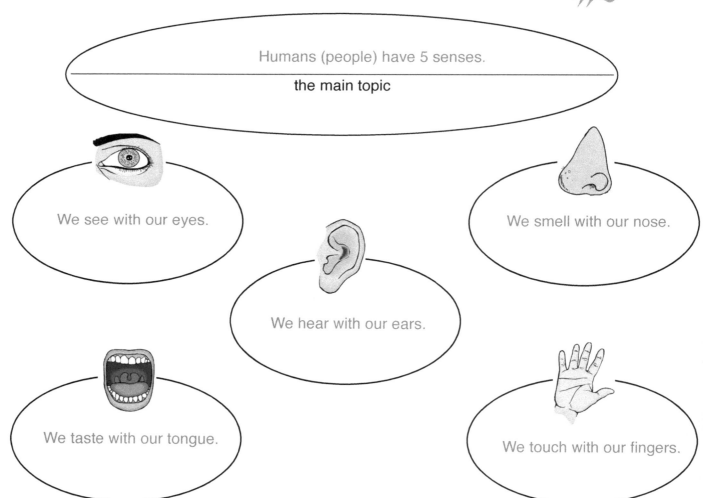

Humans (people) have 5 senses.

the main topic

We see with our eyes.

We hear with our ears.

We smell with our nose.

We taste with our tongue.

We touch with our fingers.

Name: _____

Maps

Directions: Read, or listen to the teacher read, the passage below about maps. What is the main topic of the text? Use the web to write some details about the topic.

What is a map? A map is a drawing of a place. A map shows land forms such as water, mountains, and forests. A map can also show things like railroads, parks, and schools. A map can show countries and states. A globe is a map of the Earth.   People use maps to find places and learn about different areas. You can draw your own map of your house or school. Someone who makes maps for a living is called a mapmaker, or cartographer.

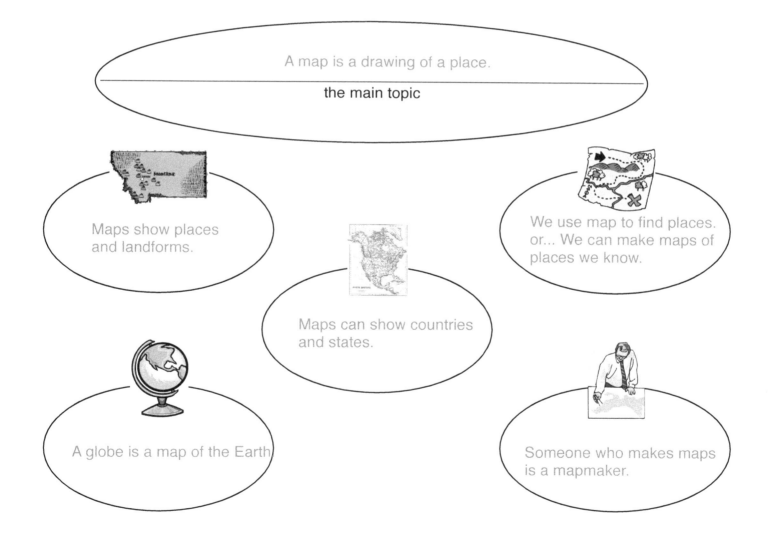

A map is a drawing of a place.

the main topic

Maps show places and landforms.

We use map to find places. or... We can make maps of places we know.

Maps can show countries and states.

A globe is a map of the Earth

Someone who makes maps is a mapmaker.

Level: Kindergarten

Name: _____

Comparing Characters

Directions: Listen to an informational story and compare two characters. How are they alike? How are they different?

<u>Different</u>

Answers vary

<u>Same</u>

<u>Different</u>

How are the two characters connected? What do they share? How are they alike?

. . . .

_____

_____

_____

_____

_____

_____

Standard: Reading I Informational Text I RI.K.3

Name: _____

Making Connections

Directions: Describe the connection between two events in a story. Listen to your teacher read The Lorax. Complete the story map. Make a connection between certain events that happen in the story.

What happens first?

What happens next?

How are these two events connected? How does one thing cause the next to happen?

Answers vary

Standard: Reading I Informational Text I RI.K.3

©http://CoreCommonStandards.com

Level: Kindergarten   Name: _____

What's That Word?

Directions: Read, or listen to, the passages below. Figure out the meaning of each underlined word by listening to the clues in each passage, looking at the picture, and thinking about what's happening.

When the caterpillar is ready to become a butterfly it makes a <u>chrysalis</u>.

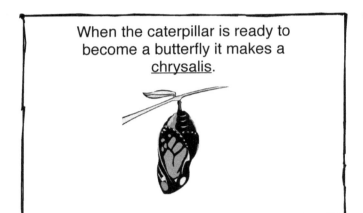

What do you think a <u>chrysalis</u> is?
_____

A place where a butterfly sleeps.
Where a butterfly is born.
Where a butterfly comes from.

 Five days after I planted my seed, it began to <u>sprout.</u>

What do you think the word <u>sprout</u> means?
_____

a growing plant. A baby plant.
It means to grow.

It was hot out so I checked the <u>thermometer</u> to see how hot.

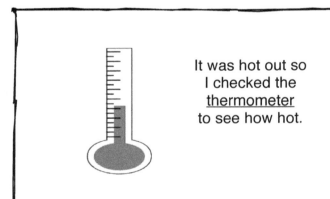

What do you think a thermometer is?
_____

A tool to show you how hot something is.

Last night we had a rain storm and bright lightning <u>struck.</u>

What do you think the word <u>struck</u> means?
_____

To get hit. To get hurt by something.

Standard: Reading I Informational Text I RI.K.4   ©http://CoreCommonStandards.com

Name: _____

Football

Directions: Read, or listen to the teacher read, the passage below about football. Write any unknown words in the box. Talk about the words you do not know with a partner or your teacher.

People have been playing football for centuries. It began in Greece and was a very rough game. Football has been played in the United States since 1869. Two colleges played together. The game we play now is safer. Players wear helmets and follow rules. Kids play now, too. People watch football on television and have parties when their teams do well.

Do you see any words that you do not know?

Write them in the space below.

Answers may vary. Expected unknown words are: centuries, Greece, rough, United States, colleges, together, safer, players, helmets, follow, rules, television, parties...

Now try to answer these questions:

Think about what is happening in the story.   What do you think the word means?

 What clues can help you?

What does the word look like?

Book Knowledge

Directions: Match the book picture to its proper name.

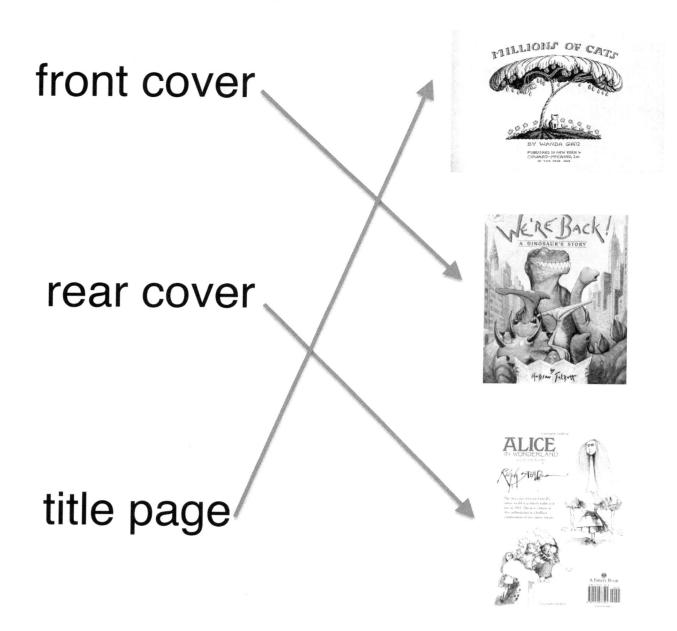

front cover

rear cover

title page

Name: _____

Book Knowledge

Directions: Choose a book. Draw what you see on the front cover, rear cover, and title page of the book.

The book I chose is: _____ The author is: _____

The illustrator is: _____

front cover	rear cover	title page
		Answers vary

Standard: Reading I Informational Text I RI.K.5

Name: _____

Illustrators

Directions: Look at the book cover illustration. Think about why the illustrator drew that picture and how it may help to tell the story.

Who is the illustrator of this book?

_____

Jessie Hartland (same as the author)

_____

_____

_____

Look at the picture on the book cover. What do you think might happen in this story?

_____

Sample answers:

_____

There is a dinosaur in the museum. The man is fixing the
dinosaur. There are bones. The man is putting the dinosaur
together. A dinosaur will come alive!

_____

_____

_____

_____

_____

How did the illustrator's drawing help you think about the story?

_____

Sample answers:

_____

I saw the bones. He looks like a doctor that fixes stuff. He is
building a dinosaur. He is putting together bones.

_____

_____

_____

_____

Standard: Reading I Informational Text I RI.K.6

Name: _____

Authors

Directions: Listen to the story *Chicka Chicka Boom Boom*. Think about what the author does to tell his story.

Who are the authors of this book?

Bill Martin Jr. and John Archambault

_____

_____

_____

_____

_____

_____

_____

Why do you think the authors wrote this story?

answers will vary

_____

_____

_____

How did the authors make this story fun to listen to or read?

answers will vary

_____

_____

What part of the authors' words did you like the best?

answers will vary

_____

_____

_____

_____

Standard: Reading I Informational Text I RI.K.6   ©http://CoreCommonStandards.com

Name: _____

Illustrations

Directions: Look at the book illustration. Think about why the illustrator drew that picture and how it may help to tell the story.

Sally felt a little lonely tonight, so she played with the one friend that never left her side.

What does this illustration say about the text?

What is Sally trying to do? _She is dressing up her dog._____

How do you know? _Dogs don't usually wear clothes._____

How does the dog feel? _He feels silly or weird. He likes it._____

How do you know? _He has a funny expression. He looks silly._____

How does Sally feel? _She is happy._____

How do you know? _She is smiling or laughing._____

How does the picture help the text make sense? _____

_It tells why Sally is dressing up her dog._____

_____

Name: _____

Illustrations

Directions: Look at the book illustration. Think about why the illustrator drew that picture and how it may help to tell the story.

Tim taught his sister, Clara, his favorite thing to do on windy days.

What does this illustration say about the text?

What is Tim teaching Clara? _Tim is teaching Clara to fly a kite._

How do you know? _They are flying kites together. Tim is older. Tim is helping her. The words tell me._

How are the kites staying in the air? _The wind is blowing. The kites are flying. They are pulling the strings._

How do you know? _It looks windy. The words said it was windy._

_____

What does the picture show that helps to tell the story? _____

The picture shows clouds and wind. The girl's dress and hair are blowing.

_____

_____

Name: _____

<u>Petey</u>

Directions: Read, or listen to the teacher read, the passage below about Petey. What are the reasons the author gives for the boy to get Petey from his aunt?

My aunt wanted to give us her dog, Petey. Mom didn't want a dog. She thought dogs were loud and a lot of work. Petey wasn't loud. He was a small dog with a little squeaky bark. He wouldn't be too much work to take care of because he was so small. Taking him for walks would be fun. And I could carry him if he got tired.

Mom said that having a dog in the house would be messy. I told mom that I would train Petey to be housebroken. I'd pick up all his dog toys, and vacuum up his hair that he sheds.

Mom said a dog needs a lot of attention. I smiled. That was the best part. I'd always have a friend that wanted to play. Mom smiled, too. The next day, we picked Petey up from my aunt's house!

What reasons in the text does the author give to support getting Petey the dog?

> Sample Answers:
> 1. Petey wasn't loud.
> 2. Taking him for walks would be fun.

> 3. I could carry him if he got tired.
> 4. Petey would be trained.
> 5. I would pick up his toys.

> 6. I would vacuum his hair.
> 7. I'd have a friend to play with.

Name: _____

Ferris Wheel

Directions: Read, or listen to the teacher read, the passage below about a ferris wheel. What are the reasons the author gives for not wanting to ride the ferris wheel?

Today we came to the amusement park. I refuse to go on the ferris wheel. I am too afraid. It is fast. It is too high. A bird might smack into me!

My brother says I am chicken. Well, I say, chickens don't like to be really high off the ground either! A ferris wheel is round. What if it falls apart and rolls away while I am on it?

My sister says I'd get to see the whole park at once. I say, I can see the same thing on the park map. I don't want to ride the ferris wheel. I think I will just wait in line for the tea cup ride.

What reasons in the text does the author give to support not riding the ferris wheel?

Sample Answers:
1. It is fast.
2. It is too high.

3. A bird might smack into me.
4. Chicken's don't like to be high off the ground, either. 5. It might roll away.
6. I can see the park map.

Level: Kindergarten

Comparing Similar Texts: *informational picture storybooks*

Directions: After reading, or listening to, two different stories about the same topic, complete the chart to identify things about the stories that are similar.

Titles	
Topic	
Illustrations _____ How are the illustrations similar?	Answers Vary
Settings _____ How are the settings similar?	

46

Standard: Reading I Informational Text I RI.K.9

Level: Kindergarten

Comparing Similar Texts: *expository*

Directions: After reading, or listening to, two different stories about the same topic, complete the chart to identify things about the stories that are similar.

Titles		
Topic		
Chapters How are the book's sections similar?	Answers Vary	
Pictures How are the illustrations, diagrams, or photographs similar?		

47

Standard: Reading I Informational Text I RI.K.9

Level: Kindergarten   Name: _____

We Read Nonfiction Together

Directions: Use this form when you meet with a group and read nonfiction text. Talk about the information and how it is presented in the book. Share ideas.

Who is in my group?	What nonfiction text are we reading? What is the topic?
Answers Vary	

Here are some things we learned about the topic.

Name: _____

What Are They Reading?

Directions: Keep track of the nonfiction text your students can read this year at grade level. Write the date each type of text was read successfully.

Name	nonfiction storybook	photo-graphic essay	auto-biography	informational book	journal/ diary

Standard: Reading I Informational Text I RI.K.10   ©http://CoreCommonStandards.com

Name: _____

I Can Read

I can read from left to right.

Directions: Read the sentences below. Start at the left and move to the right.

READING PRACTICE

The dog wants to eat his food now.

→

I can jump over the box on the floor.

→

My mom and dad took me to the zoo.

→

We had lots of fun at the zoo with the class.

→

I know that spaces go between words.

Directions: Rewrite the sentences below so that they have spaces.

Thecatwentinthebox.

The cat went in the box.

CanIhavethatcake?

Can I have that cake?

Level: Kindergarten

Name: _____

I Know my Letters!

I know my upper- and lower-case letters.

Directions: Circle all of the upper-case letters. Cross-out all of the lower-case letters.

A₁ O₁ h₄ c₃ B₃

F₄ D₂ H₄ o₁ v₄

t₁ C₃ b₃

k₅ a₁ R₁ s₁

K₅ N M₃

Write the missing letters.

D, E ,F, G ,H,I, J ,K, L , M

Write the missing letters.

p q ,r, s ,t, u ,v,w, x , y ,z

Standard: Reading I Foundational Skills I RF.K.1

©http://CoreCommonStandards.com

Name: _____

Sounds

Directions: Look at the pictures below. Say the words. Think about beginning, middle, and ending sounds. Choose the word that matches each pictures. Trace the correct word.

	log	(dog)	dot
	(sun)	fun	sub
	bat	(cat)	can
	bet	bun	(bus)
	peg	(pig)	wig
	(jet)	jam	bet

Name: _____

Complete the Words

Directions: Look at the pictures below. Say the words. Think about beginning, middle, and ending sounds. Complete the words for each picture.

	m o p
	p i n
	r u n
	n e t
	c a r
	t u b

Name: _____

Long and Short Spellings

Directions: Look at the pictures below and read the words for each picture. Circle the words and pictures correctly by following the key.

long a : blue   long e : red
short a : green   short e : brown

leaf RED	cat GREEN	jay BLUE	red BROWN
clap GREEN	clam GREEN	cheese RED	snail BLUE
cake BLUE	hen BROWN	flag GREEN	bat GREEN
feet BLUE	fan GREEN	bread BROWN	key RED
jet BROWN	thread BROWN	steak BLUE	egg BROWN
sack GREEN	thief RED	chain BLUE	snake BLUE

Standard: Reading I Foundational Skills I RF.K.3

©http://CoreCommonStandards.com

Level: Kindergarten   Name: _____

Long and Short Spellings

Directions: Look at the pictures below and read the words for each picture. Circle the words and pictures correctly by following the key.

long i : red   long o : orange   long u and oo : blue
short i : brown   short o : purple   short u : green

kite RED	fruit BLUE	lip BROWN	screw BLUE
jug GREEN	rope ORANGE	box PURPLE	fight RED
toad ORANGE	drum GREEN	pool BLUE	snow ORANGE
flute BLUE	pie RED	ship BROWN	soup BLUE
stop PURPLE	glue BLUE	frog PURPLE	bus GREEN
toe ORANGE	cry RED	mule BLUE	bug GREEN

Standard: Reading I Foundational Skills I RF.K.3   ©http://CoreCommonStandards.com

Level: Kindergarten

Name: _____

I Can Read

Directions: Read the text below. Remember to start at the left and move to the right. Stop at the periods and think about the words.

The Dog

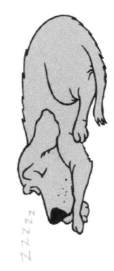

Dog can play.

Dog can sleep.

Dog is brown and big.

©http://CoreCommonStandards.com

The Ant

Ant can run and he can jump.

Ant is black and small.

☐ I read The Ant.

☐ I read The Dog.

Standard: Reading I Foundational Skills I RF.K.4

56

Name: _____

I Can Read

Directions: Read the text below. Remember to start at the left and move to the right. Stop at the periods and think about the words.

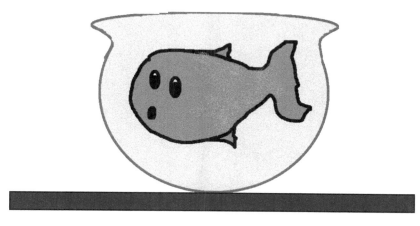

Fish

Fish is little.
He swims.
He likes to eat green plants.
Fish is good.
Fish is red.
Fish is in my room.

What color is Fish? <u>red _____</u>

What does Fish do? <u>swim _____</u>

Name: _____

Writing About a Book

Directions: Draw, write, or tell about your favorite book and why you like it.

answers vary

Standard: Reading I Writing I W.K.1
Graphics (c) ScrappinDoodles

Name: _____

Writing About a Character

Directions: Draw, write, or tell about a favorite character from a book you like.

answers vary

_____
- - - - - - - - - - - - - - - - - - - -
_____
- - - - - - - - - - - - - - - - - - - -
_____
- - - - - - - - - - - - - - - - - - - -
_____
- - - - - - - - - - - - - - - - - - - -
_____

Name: _____

Writing About a Topic

Directions: Choose a topic that you are interested in and know something about. Draw, write, or tell about the topic. Tell what you are writing about and give some information.

answers vary

Name: _____

Writing About Animals

Directions: Choose an animal that you are interested in and know something about. Draw, write, or tell about the animal. Tell what animal you are writing about and give some information.

answers vary

Name: _____

Writing About Me

Directions: Choose an event that happened in your life. Draw, write, or tell about something that you remember from your own life. Tell the story in order. How did you feel?

answers vary

_____
- -
_____
_____
- -
_____
_____
- -
_____
_____
- -

Level: Kindergarten   Name: _____

Writing About School

Directions: Choose an event that happened in your school. Draw, write, or tell about something that you remember from a day at school. Tell the events in order. How did you feel?

answers vary

_____

- -

_____

- -

_____

- -

_____

- -

_____

Standard: Reading | Writing | W.K.3
Graphics (c) ScrappinDoodles   ©http://CoreCommonStandards.com

Name: _____ .

Work In Progress

Directions: Write about something that makes you happy. Share your writing with a friend. Listen to questions and suggestions your friend has and work together to make your writing better.

answers vary

Name: _____

Working Together

Directions: Work with a partner to improve upon your writing. Share your writing and listen to your partner's ideas.

I am working together with...

answers vary

_____

My writing is titled...

_____

Something I added to my writing...

_____

_____

Something my partner liked...

_____

_____

Something I liked...

_____

_____

Standard: Reading I Writing I W.K.5
Graphics (c) ScrappinDoodles

©http://CoreCommonStandards.com

Other Ways to Write

Directions: Today, many people use digital tools to write. Write your story using the computer and other digital tools.

I want to write about...

answers vary

_____

I am going to use a computer to type my story.

I want to add pictures to my story by using...

a. *digital camera*, b. *scanner*, c. *clipart website*.

I will share my writing by...

a. *printing my story*,
b. *emailing it to my classmates*,
c. *presenting it using a projector*

Something new I learned using these tools is...

_____
_____
_____

Standard: Reading I Writing I W.K.6
Graphics (c) ScrappinDoodles

Level: Kindergarten   Name: _____

Using Digital Resources

Directions: Today, many people use digital tools to write. Use this checklist to record what digital skills each student can perform.

Digital Skill	Date	Success
Can turn on a computer.		
Can shut down a computer.		
Uses a mouse well. (Can double-click; move cursor to desired place; scroll if available.)		
Knows where most common characters are on keyboard.		
Can log in and out of programs.		
Can change the font or size of font.		
Knows how to use space bar; back space; delete; and return.		
Can add a graphic.		
Can drag and drop an item.		
Can copy/paste an item.		
Can save a file.		
Can print work.		

Standard: Reading I Writing I W.K.6   ©http://CoreCommonStandards.com

Name: _____

Research Together

Directions: Work with a partner, or a group, to research a topic. Use several books to gather information about your topic. Work together to read and write about the topic you chose.

Our Topic:

answers vary

_____

Books we read:

_____

_____

_____

Here are some things we found out about

_____ :

_____

_____

_____

_____

_____

Name: _____

Research Together

Directions: Work with a partner to explore several books by your favorite author and write what you think about each book.

Book Title	What I Think About The Book
answers vary	

Name: _____

My Experience

Directions: Think about a time in your life you want to tell about. Think about where you were, who you were with, what you did, and how you felt. Write about that time.

My Story

answers vary

_____
- -
_____
- -
_____
- -
_____
- -
_____
- -
_____

Name: _____

Answering a Question

Directions: You have a question to answer. Think about the question. Use resources your teacher provides to find information to help you answer the question. Write your answer below.

paste question here

I am using resources my teacher gave me.
This is some information I found to help me answer the question.

answers vary

Here is my answer to the question.

_____
- -
_____
- -
_____

Standard: Reading I Writing I W.K.8
Graphics (c) ScrappinDoodles

©http://CoreCommonStandards.com

Level: Kindergarten   Name: _____

Small Group Discussions

Directions: When we meet for discussions in Kindergarten, we follow group rules.

 Take Turns

 Listen To Others

 Stay on Topic

 Respect Others' Ideas

 Participate

Name: _____

Understanding a Text

Directions: Listen to your teacher read a story to the class. Think about the story and write a question you have. Draw a picture about the story. Then, share your paper with the class.

My teacher read a story to us today called: _____

_____

Here is one question I want to ask about the story: _____

_____

Here is a picture that tells about the story:

answers vary

Now, read your question to the class and tell about your picture.

Standard: Reading I Speaking & Listening I SL.K.2
Graphics (c) ScrappinDoodles

Name: _____

Asking Questions

Directions: Students should ask questions in order to seek help, get information, or clarify something that is not understood. Take anecdotal notes when you hear students asking these kinds of questions.

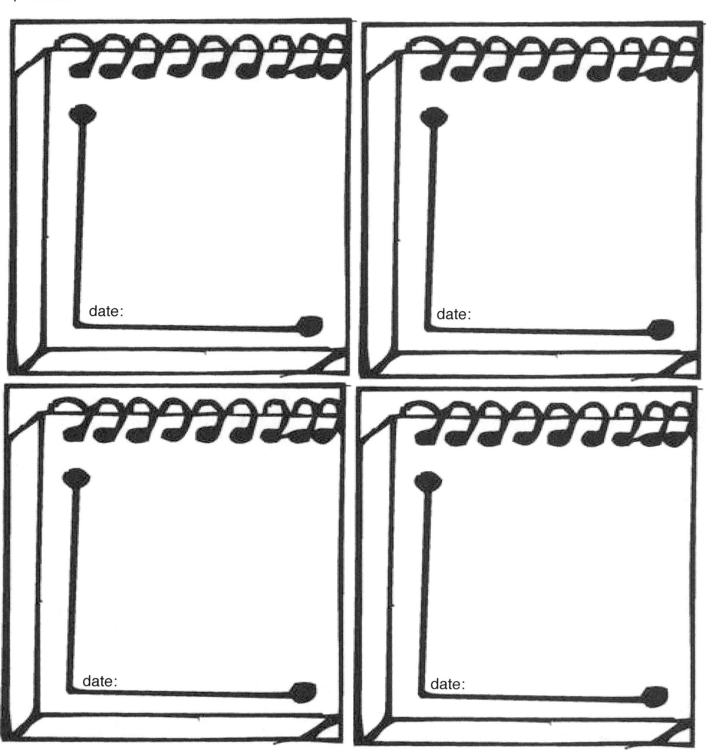

date:

date:

date:

date:

Name: _____

Describing Orally

Directions: Draw a picture of someone you know, something you do, or somewhere you have been. Describe your drawing to the class.

I can describe something I do, someone I know, or somewhere I have been. Here is a picture.

answers vary

This is a picture of _____

_____

Now, share your description with the class.

Standard: Reading I Speaking & Listening I SL.K.4
Graphics (c) ScrappinDoodles

©http://CoreCommonStandards.com

Name: _____

Adding Details

Directions: Give a description and then add detail to the story by drawing a picture.

Give a description of an event, a person, a place, or a thing you know.

Add more detail by drawing a picture.

Tell about what you drew. How does it add detail to your description?

answers varu

This is a picture of _____

_____

Standard: Reading I Speaking & Listening I SL.K.5
Graphics (c) ScrappinDoodles   ©http://CoreCommonStandards.com

Level: Kindergarten

Name: _____

Student Speak

Directions: Students should speak audibly and express thoughts, feelings, and ideas clearly. Take anecdotal notes when you hear students speaking with these qualities.

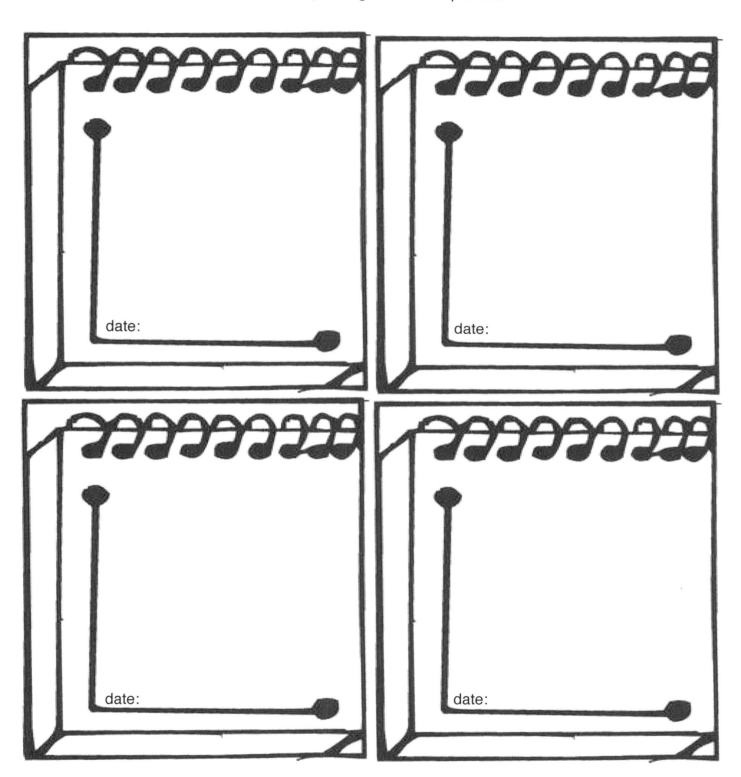

Standard: Reading I Speaking & Listening I SL.K.6

©http://CoreCommonStandards.com

Name: _____

Sentences

Directions: Look at the pictures below. Write a sentence for each picture. Think about what sentences need. Don't forget a capital letter, end mark, and spaces.

The boys are standing with their friends.
The boy is with his friends.
The boys are on a team.

The girl has paint on her hands.
The girl has paint on her apron.
The girl has paint on the floor.

The woman has ice cream in a bowl.
The women put ice cream in their bowls.
There are cherries on top of the ice cream.
There are bananas in the bowl.

Name: _____

The Alphabet

Directions: Write the capital or lower-case letters for each letter shown.

A	a ___	H	h ___	P	p ___	R	r ___
Z	z ___	F	f ___	H	h ___	I	i ___
Y	y ___	S	s ___	B	b ___	Q	q ___
R	r ___	T	t ___	Q	q ___	A	a ___
J	j ___	G	g ___	N	n ___	T	t ___
V	v ___	X	x ___	S	s ___	D	d ___
O	o ___	M	m ___	E	e ___	U	u ___
L	I ___	K	k ___	P	p ___	U	u ___

Name: _____

Questions

Directions: Use the words *who, what, where, when, why* and *how* to ask oral questions about the pictures shown below.

| who? | what? | where? | when? | why? | how? |

Name: _____

Fixing Sentences

Directions: Read the sentences below. Give each sentence a capital letter at the beginning and the correct punctuation at the end. { .   !   ? }

1	we go to school on the bus We go to school on the bus.
2	i read a book in my bed I read a book in my bed.
3	can we go to the park today Can we go to the park today?
4	look at all the ants on the cake Look at all the ants on the cake! (or .)
5	i want to eat some popcorn now I want to eat some popcorn now. (or !)
6	dad and mom have a gift for me Dad and mom have a gift for me!
7	what color is that dog What color is that dog?
8	the tree in my yard has apples The tree in my yard has apples.

Name: _____

Beginning Sounds

Directions: Circle the correct beginning sound for each picture bellow.

p r (h)	(v) b t	(z) r k
m (c) p	f (s) w	l p (b)
(b) c m	l w (b)	(m) z d
g (c) r	t s (f)	m (k) d

Level: Kindergarten

Name: _____

Spelling Words

Directions: Look at the pictures below. Write a word for each picture.

hat	sun	ladle, scoop, dipper, pan, measuring cup…
ham, roast, meat	bed	pig
nut, walnut	bib	pen, ink pen, ballpen

Standard: Reading | Language | L.K.2   ©http://CoreCommonStandards.com

Name: _____

Knowing Words

Directions: Circle the correct word for each picture. The words sound the same but have different meanings.

(bear) bare	dear (deer)	sale (sail)
read (red)	not (knot)	right (write)
to (two)	(eye) I	made (maid)
(hi) high	(hay) hey	rows (rose)

Name: _____

Meeting Unknown Words

Directions: While reading a new story to the class, use this sheet to pull out unknown words from the story. Using illustrations, explanatory phrases, props, and voice inflection, help students understand the words' meanings.

Book Title:_____answers vary_____

New vocabulary words:	What do you think the word means?

Name: _____

New Meanings

Directions: While reading a new story to the class, use this sheet to identify known words that may have different meanings.

Story: _____	**Story:** _____
In this story, what does the word _____ mean?	In this story, what does the word _____ mean?
Which picture shows what the word _____ means?	Which picture shows what the word _____ means? answers vary
In this story, what does the word _____ mean?	In this story, what does the word _____ mean?
Which picture shows what the word _____ means?	Which picture shows what the word _____ means?

Standard: Reading I Language I L.K.4

Name: _____

Matching Opposites

Directions: Read the words on the left and find its opposite match on the right. Draw a line to connect the two.

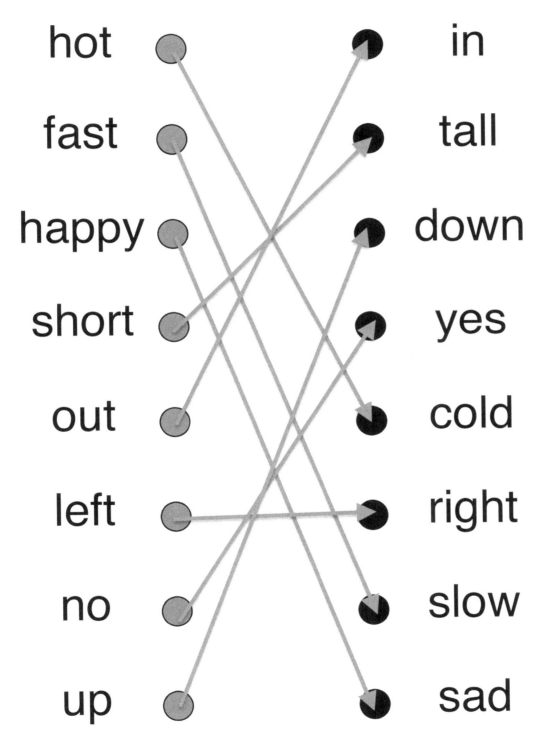

hot   in

fast   tall

happy   down

short   yes

out   cold

left   right

no   slow

up   sad

Name: _____

Categories

Directions: Match the pictures to their correct categories.

Fruit = apple, strawberries, blueberries, lime, grapes, banana
Shapes = triangle, rectangle, cube, and circle
Animals = shark, bird, cow, fly, spider, squirrel
Plants = tree, cactus, branch with nuts, fern (hanging plant)

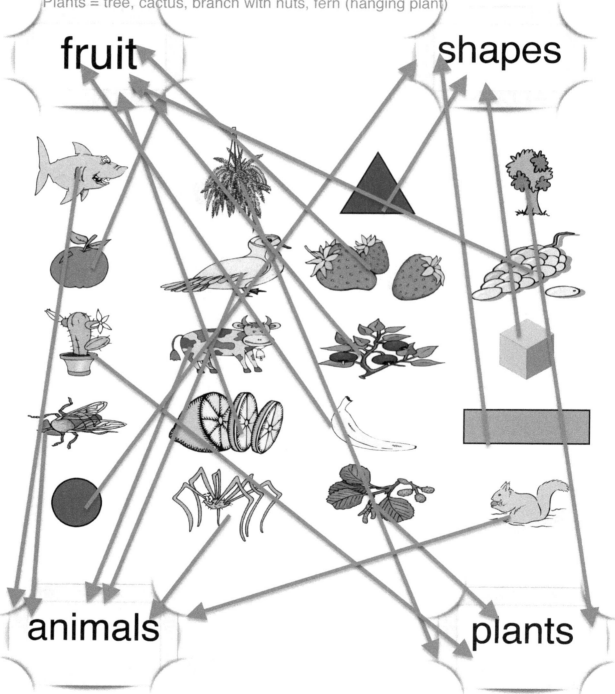

Name: _____

Verbs!

Directions: Verbs are words that describe an action; something you can do. Read the verbs below. Act out the verbs to show you know what they mean. Write a sentence for each verb.

climb	Sample Sentences 1. The man is climbing a rope.
run	2. The girl is running.
jump	3. The boy is jumping
cut	4. The scissors are cutting paper.
clap	5. The boy and girl are clapping.
write	6. The crab is writing.

Name: __VOCAB PRACTICE__

Wonderful Words: Arthur's TV Trouble

Directions: Use the words from *Arthur's TV Trouble* by Marc Brown to respond to the story, answer questions, and retell the events. Read the words together. Think about what they mean. You can also place the words in alphabetical order, sort them by part-of-speech, or use them in sentences.

announcer 	Treat Timer 
machine 	expensive 
recycled 	newspaper 
assemble 	commercials 

Standard: Reading I Language I L.K.6
Graphics (c) KidsEconPosters.com

©http://CoreCommonStandards.com

Name: _____

Wonderful Words:
The Day Jimmy's Boa Ate the Wash

Directions: Use the words from *The Day Jimmy's Boa Ate the Wash* by Trinka Hankes Noble to respond to the story, answer questions, and retell the events. Read the words together. Think about what they mean. You can also place the words in alphabetical order, sort them by part-of-speech, or use them in sentences.

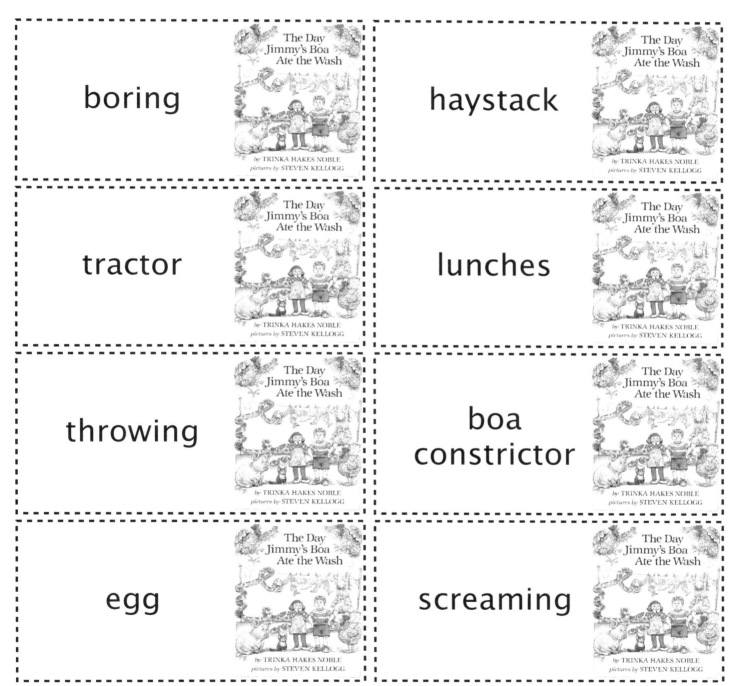

boring

haystack

tractor

lunches

throwing

boa constrictor

egg

screaming

Standard: Reading I Language I L.K.6
Graphics (c) TheReadingNook.com

©http://CoreCommonStandards.com

Name: _____

Wonderful Words:
The Paper Bag Princess

Directions: Use the words from *TThe Paper Bag Princess* by Robert N. Munsch to respond to the story, answer questions, and retell the events. Read the words together. Think about what they mean. You can also place the words in alphabetical order, sort them by part-of-speech, or use them in sentences.

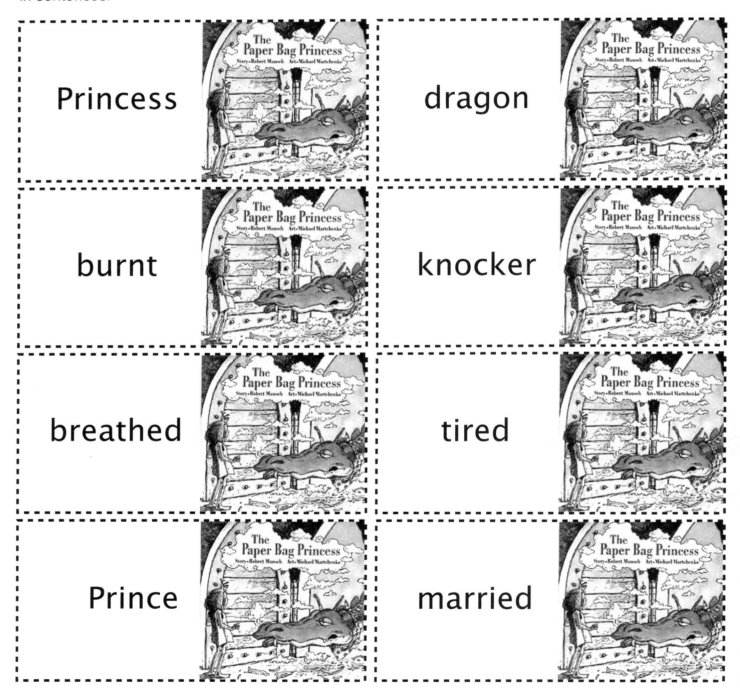

Princess	dragon
breathed	tired
burnt	knocker
Prince	married

Common Core State Standards

Kindergarten Worksheets Common Core Workbook

Grade K

• Math Standards

Worksheets that teach every Common Core Standard!

Name:

I Can Count to One Hundred!

Directions: Start at 0 and count to 100 by **ONES**. Then, close your eyes and try again!

0	1	2	3	4	5	6	7	8	9
10	11	12	13	14	15	16	17	18	19
20	21	22	23	24	25	26	27	28	29
30	31	32	33	34	35	36	37	38	39
40	41	42	43	44	45	46	47	48	49
50	51	52	53	54	55	56	57	58	59
60	61	62	63	64	65	66	67	68	69
70	71	72	73	74	75	76	77	78	79
80	81	82	83	84	85	86	87	88	89
90	91	92	93	94	95	96	97	98	99
100									

Today, ___/___/___, I counted to _____!

Today, ___/___/___, I counted to _____!

Today, ___/___/___, I counted to _____!

Standard: Math I Counting and Cardinality I K.CC.1

Name: _____

I Can Count to One Hundred!

Directions: Start at 0 and count to 100 by **TENS**. Then, close your eyes and try it again!

0	1	2	3	4	5	6	7	8	9
10	11	12	13	14	15	16	17	18	19
20	21	22	23	24	25	26	27	28	29
30	31	32	33	34	35	36	37	38	39
40	41	42	43	44	45	46	47	48	49
50	51	52	53	54	55	56	57	58	59
60	61	62	63	64	65	66	67	68	69
70	71	72	73	74	75	76	77	78	79
80	81	82	83	84	85	86	87	88	89
90	91	92	93	94	95	96	97	98	99
100									

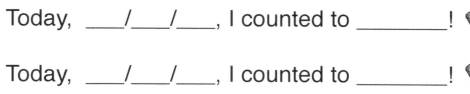

Today, ___/___/___, I counted to _____!

Today, ___/___/___, I counted to _____!

Today, ___/___/___, I counted to _____!

Standard: Math I Counting and Cardinality I K.CC.1

©www.CoreCommonStandards.com

Name: _____

I Can Count Starting at ANY Number!

Directions: Say each number out loud. Then, count forward by **ONES**.
(Teachers, use this sheet to record student counting.)

0	1	2	3	4	5	6	7	8	9	10
1	… count up from ones starting at the numbers on the left.									
2										
3										
4										
5										
6										
7										
8										
9										
10										
11										
12										
13										
14										
15										
16										
17										
18										
19										
20										

Standard: Math I Counting and Cardinality I K.CC.2

©www.CoreCommonStandards.com

Level: Kindergarten   Name: _____

I Can Count Starting at ANY Number!

Directions: Say each number out loud. Then, count forward by **ONES**.
(Teachers, use this sheet to record student counting.)

23	24	25	26	27	28	29	30	31	32	33
45	... count up from ones starting at the numbers on the left.								
72									
66									
41									
83									
22									
19									
60									
57									
35									
90									
28									
48									
64									
55									
86									
39									
61									
77									
82									

Standard: Math | Counting and Cardinality | K.CC.2   ©www.CoreCommonStandards.com

Name: _____

Can You Write Your Numbers?

Directions: Count the dots. Write the number for how many dots you counted.

○○○○○○○○○○	○○○	○○○○○○○○○○ ○○○○○○○○
10	3	18
○○○○○○○○○○ ○	○○○○○○○○○	○○
11	9	2
○○○○○○○○○○ ○○○○○○○○○	○○○○○○	○○○○○○○○○○ ○○○○○○○○○○
19	6	20
○○○○○○○○○○ ○○○○○	○○○○○○○○	○○○○○○○○○○ ○○
15	8	12
○○○○○○○○○○ ○○○○○○	○○○○○○○○○○ ○○○	○○○○○○○○○○ ○○○○○○○
16	13	17
○○○○○	○○○○○○○○○○ ○○○○	○○○○
5	14	4
○	○○○○○○○	
1	7	0

Standard: Math I Counting and Cardinality I K.CC.3

Name: _____

Can You Write Your Numbers?

<u>Directions:</u> Count the squares. Write the number for how many squares you counted.

□□□□□	□□□□□□□□□□	□□□□□□□□□□ □□□□□
5	10	15
□□□□□□□□□□ □□	□□□□□□□□□□ □	□□
12	11	2
□□□□□□	□□□□□□□□□□ □□□□□□□□□	□□□□□□□□□□ □□□
6	19	13
□□□□□□□□□□ □□□□□□□□□	□□□□□□□□□□ □□□□□□□□□□	□□□□□□□□□
19	20	9
□□□□□□□	□□□□□□□□□□ □□□□□□□	□□□□□□□□□□ □□□□
7	17	14
□□□	□□□□□□□□□□ □□□□□□	□□□□□□□□
3	16	8
□		□□□□
1	0	4

Name: _____

Touch and Count

<u>Directions:</u> Touch each picture and count the objects in order. Then, say the total amount.
Hint: The last number said tells the total number of objects counted.
(Teachers, you may use this sheet to record student counting.)

apple	apple	apple	apple	apple	apple	apple					7
football	football	football	football	football	football	football	football	football	football		10
tree	tree	tree	tree	tree							5
earth	earth	earth	earth	earth	earth	earth	earth				8
lemon	lemon	lemon	lemon	lemon	lemon						6
pumpkin	pumpkin	pumpkin	pumpkin	pumpkin	pumpkin	pumpkin	pumpkin	pumpkin	pumpkin	pumpkin	11
die	die	die									3
tooth	tooth	tooth	tooth	tooth	tooth	tooth	tooth	tooth			9
flower	flower	flower	flower								4
moon	moon										2

Standard: Math | Counting and Cardinality | K.CC.4   ©www.CoreCommonStandards.com

Name: _____

Touch and Count

Directions: Touch each picture and count the objects in any order. Then, say the total amount.
Hint: The last number said tells the total number of objects counted.
(Teachers, you may use this sheet to record student counting.)

3	4	5
8	12	7
1	6	2
10	9	11

Standard: Math I Counting and Cardinality I K.CC.4   ©www.CoreCommonStandards.com

Name: _____

How Many?

Directions: Touch each picture and count the objects.
Then, tell how many of each object you counted

1.

7

_____

2.

8

_____

3.

9

_____

4.

6

_____

5.

8

_____

6.

6

_____

Standard: Math | Counting and Cardinality | K.CC.5

©www.CoreCommonStandards.com

Name: _____

How Many?

Directions: Touch each picture and count the objects.
Then, tell how many of each object you counted.

1.

19
_____

2.

12
_____

3.

15
_____

4.

10
_____

5.

14
_____

6.

18
_____

Standard: Math | Counting and Cardinality | K.CC.5

©www.CoreCommonStandards.com

Name: ___answers vary___

How Many?

<u>Directions:</u> Arrange up to 20 objects in different ways, such as a line, a rectangle, or a circle. Or, arrange as many as 10 things in a scattered configuration.
Then, ask the student, "How many objects are there?"

Type of Object	Number of Objects	Configuration	Student Response
Example Cheerios	Example 8	Example Rectangle	Example Student placed objects in 2 groups of 4

Comments:

Standard: Math I Counting and Cardinality I K.CC.5   ©www.CoreCommonStandards.com

Name: ___answers vary___

How Many?

Directions: Tell the student a number from 1 to 20. Have the student use objects to count out that number.

Number Given	Object Used	Configuration Used	Student Response
Example 14	Example Crayons	Example Line	Example Student lined up the crayons in a row

Comments:

Standard: Math I Counting and Cardinality I K.CC.5

Name: <u>answers vary</u>

Greater Than, Less Than, Equal To?

<u>Directions:</u> Using objects, create 2 groups of either different or equal values. Ask the student to compare the two groups by using matching and counting strategies. Ask student if one group is greater than, less than, or equal to the other.

Group 1	Group 2	Student Response	Student Data	
Example 7	Example 5	Example 7 > 5	Correct ✓	Incorrect
			Correct	Incorrect
			Correct	Incorrect
			Correct	Incorrect
			Correct	Incorrect
			Correct	Incorrect
			Correct	Incorrect
			Correct	Incorrect
			Correct	Incorrect
			Correct	Incorrect

Comments:

Standard: Math I Counting and Cardinality I K.CC.6   ©www.CoreCommonStandards.com

Name: _____

Greater Than, Less Than, Equal To?

Directions: Have the student look at the groups of dots below.
Ask the student to compare Group A with Group B.
Then, ask the question, "Is Group A **More Than**, **Less Than**, or **Equal To** Group B?

Group A	Group B	Student Response
		equal to
		greater than
		less than
		greater than

Comments:

Standard: Math I Counting and Cardinality I K.CC.6   ©www.CoreCommonStandards.com

Greater Than, Less Than, Equal To?

Directions: Have the student look at the groups of dots below.
Ask the student to compare Group A with Group B.
Then, ask the question, "Is Group A **More Than**, **Less Than**, or **Equal To** Group B?

Group A	Group B	Student Response
		greater than
		greater than
		less than
		equal to

Comments:

Name: _____

Greater Than, Less Than, Equal To?

Directions: Have the student look at the numbers below.
Ask the student to compare Number A with Number B.
Then, ask the question, "Is the First Number **More Than**, **Less Than**, or **Equal To** the Second Number?

First Number	Second Number	Student Response
6	3	greater than
7	10	less than
2	5	less than
9	9	equal to

Comments:

Standard: Math I Counting and Cardinality I K.CC.7   ©www.CoreCommonStandards.com

Level: Kindergarten   Name: _____

Greater Than, Less Than, Equal To?

<u>Directions:</u> Have the student look at the numbers below.
Ask the student to compare Number A with Number B.
Then, ask the question, "Is the First Number **More Than**, **Less Than**, or **Equal To** the Second Number?

Number A	Number B	Student Response
7	8	less than
2	2	equal to
10	1	greater than
4	6	less than

Comments:

Name: _____

Greater Than, Less Than, Equal To?

Directions: Look at the pairs of numbers below. Circle the greater number with blue. Circle the smaller number with red. If the two numbers are equal, circle them both with green.

red	blue		blue	red
5	9		4	1

red	blue		green	green
2	3		3	3

blue	red		red	blue
8	2		7	10

green	green		blue	red
4	4		5	2

blue	red		red	blue
10	6		7	9

green	green		green	green
5	5		6	6

red	blue		blue	red
3	8		8	1

Comments:

Standard: Math | Counting and Cardinality | K.CC.7   ©www.CoreCommonStandards.com

Name: _answers vary_

Addition Dice Game

Directions: Have the student roll 10-sided dice or cut out the numbers below and draw from a hat. Use the numbers to fill in the spaces below. Ask the student to show how to add the numbers together by using objects, fingers, mental images, drawings, sounds, acting it out, explaining in words, or writing an addition equation.

0 1 2 3 4 5

6 7 8 9 10

Standard: Math | Operations & Algebraic Thinking | K.OA.1   ©www.CoreCommonStandards.com

Name: _answers vary_

Subtraction Dice Game

Directions: Have the student roll 10-sided dice or cut out the numbers below and draw from a hat. Use the numbers to fill in the spaces below. Ask the student to show how to subtract the numbers by using objects, fingers, mental images, drawings, sounds, acting it out, explaining in words, or writing a subtraction equation.

```
┌──────────────────────┬──────────────────────┐
│  ┌────┐    ┌────┐     │  ┌────┐    ┌────┐     │
│  │    │    │    │     │  │    │    │    │     │
│  └────┘    └────┘     │  └────┘    └────┘     │
│                       │                       │
├──────────────────────┼──────────────────────┤
│  ┌────┐    ┌────┐     │  ┌────┐    ┌────┐     │
│  │    │    │    │     │  │    │    │    │     │
│  └────┘    └────┘     │  └────┘    └────┘     │
│                       │                       │
└──────────────────────┴──────────────────────┘
```

0   1   2   3   4   5

6   7   8   9   10

Name: _____

Addition Word Problems

Directions: Read the addition word problems. Use objects or the spaces below to draw pictures that represent each problem. Then, complete the equation with the correct answer.

---

4 ducks were in the pond. 3 more ducks came to the pond. How many total ducks were in the pond?

$$4 + 3 = \underline{\,7\,}$$

---

3 apples were in the basket. 3 more apples were put into the basket. How many apples were there in all?

$$\underline{3} + \underline{3} = \underline{6}$$

---

6 boys were in the room. 2 more boys came into the room. How many boys were there in all?

$$\underline{6} + \underline{2} = \underline{8}$$

---

1 turtle was swimming. 3 more turtles started swimming. How many turtles were swimming in all?

$$\underline{1} + \underline{3} = \underline{4}$$

---

5 girls went to the mall. 5 more girls went to the mall. How many total girls were at the mall?

$$\underline{5} + \underline{5} = \underline{10}$$

---

2 chairs were around the table. 4 more chairs were placed around the table. How many total chairs were around the table?

$$\underline{2} + \underline{4} = \underline{6}$$

Name: _____

Subtraction Word Problems

Directions: Read the subtraction word problems. Use objects or the spaces below to draw pictures that represent each problem. Then, complete the equation with the correct answer..

8 ducks were in the pond. 3 ducks flew away. How many ducks were left in the pond?

$$8 - 3 = \underline{5}$$

6 apples were in the basket. 3 apples were given away. How many apples were left in the basket?

$$\underline{6} - \underline{3} = \underline{3}$$

6 boys were in the room. 2 boys left the room. How many boys were still in the room?

$$\underline{6} - \underline{2} = \underline{4}$$

3 turtles were swimming in the water. 1 turtle went on land. How many turtles left swimming in the water?

$$\underline{3} - \underline{1} = \underline{2}$$

7 girls went to the mall. 2 girls had to go home early. How many girls were left at the mall?

$$\underline{7} - \underline{2} = \underline{5}$$

6 chairs were around the table. 4 chairs were taken away. How many chairs were left around the table?

$$\underline{6} - \underline{4} = \underline{2}$$

Standard: Math | Operations & Algebraic Thinking | K.OA.2   ©www.CoreCommonStandards.com

Name: _____

Finding Other Names

Directions: Find the matching number pairs for the numbers the cats are holding. Write the number pairs (addition equations) in the spaces below.

1+0, 0+1

1+1, 0+2, 2+0

2+1, 0+3, 1+2, 3+0

3+1, 1+3, 4+0, 2+2, 0+4

2+1	1+0	3+1	0+3	0+1
1+3	4+0	2+2	2+0	1+1
	0+2	1+2	3+0	0+4

Standard: Math I Operations & Algebraic Thinking I K.OA.3   ©www.CoreCommonStandards.com

Name: _____

Breaking Down Numbers

Directions: Find the matching number pairs for the numbers the cats are holding.
Use the spaces below to write the number pairs (addition equations) that equal the numbers.

1+4

2+4, 6+0, 3+3

4+3, 3+4

1+8, 5+3, 3+5, 4+4

1+4	2+4	6+0	1+7	5+3
3+3	4+3	3+5	3+4	4+4

Name: _____

Breaking Down Numbers

<u>Directions:</u> Find the matching number pairs for the numbers the cats are holding. Use the spaces below to write the number pairs (addition equations) that equal the numbers.

5

2+3

6

5+1, 1+5

7

6+1, 7+0, 5+2, 1+6

8

7+1, 8+0, 0+8

| 5+1 | 6+1 | 7+1 | 7+0 | 8+0 |
| 5+2 | 2+3 | 0+8 | 1+5 | 1+6 |

Name: _____

Breaking Down Numbers

Directions: Find the matching number pairs for the numbers the cats are holding.
Use the spaces below to write the number pairs (addition equations) that equal the numbers.

5

5+0, 4+1, 3+2, 0+5

6

4+2, 0+6

7

2+5, 0+7

8

6+2, 2+6

5+0	4+1	3+2	6+2	0+5
2+5	4+2	0+6	0+7	2+6

Level: Kindergarten   Name: _____

Breaking Down Numbers

Directions: Find the matching number pairs for the numbers the cats are holding.
Use the spaces below to write the number pairs (addition equations) that equal the numbers.

4+5, 3+6, 7+2,
2+7, 1+8, 8+1

5+5, 6+4, 4+6, 2+8

5+5   6+4   4+5   4+6   3+6

2+8   7+2   2+7   1+8   8+1

Name: _____

Breaking Down Numbers

Directions: Find the matching number pairs for the numbers the cats are holding.
Use the spaces below to write the number pairs (addition equations) that equal the numbers.

9+0, 6+3, 0+9, 5+4

1+9, 10+0, 7+3,
3+7, 9+1, 8+2,
0+10

1+9   9+0   10+0   7+3

3+7   6+3   9+1   0+9

5+4   8+2   0+10

Name: _____

Breaking The Numbers Apart

<u>Directions:</u> Ask the student to break apart the numbers into pairs.
Have the student show 2 ways to decompose each number. (Example: 5 = 2 + 3 and 5 = 4 + 1)
Record your work with a picture and/or an equation. You can use objects to help you.

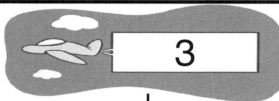

3

<u>one way</u>   <u>another way</u>

Possible Answers for 3 = 0+3, 1+2, 2+1, 3+0

<u>Equation:</u>   3 = ___ + ___   <u>Equation:</u>   3 = ___ + ___

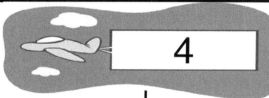

4

<u>one way</u>   <u>another way</u>

Possible Answers for 4 = 0+4, 1+3, 2+2, 3+1, 4+0

<u>Equation:</u>   4 = ___ + ___   <u>Equation:</u>   4 = ___ + ___

Standard: Math | Operations & Algebraic Thinking | K.OA.3   ©www.CoreCommonStandards.com

Name: _____

Breaking The Numbers Apart

<u>Directions:</u> Ask the student to break apart the numbers into pairs.
Have the student show 2 ways to decompose each number. (Example: 5 = 2 + 3 and 5 = 4 + 1)
Record your work with a picture and/or an equation. You can use objects to help you.

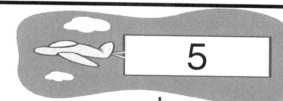

5

<u>one way</u>

<u>another way</u>

Possible Answers for 5 = 0+5, 1+4, 2+3, 3+2, 4+1, 5+0

<u>Equation:</u>   5 = ___ + ___

<u>Equation:</u>   5 = ___ + ___

6

<u>one way</u>

<u>another way</u>

Possible Answers for 6 = 0+6, 1+5, 2+4, 3+3, 4+2, 5+1, 6+0

<u>Equation:</u>   6 = ___ + ___

<u>Equation:</u>   6 = ___ + ___

Standard: Math | Operations & Algebraic Thinking | K.OA.3   ©www.CoreCommonStandards.com

Name: _____

Breaking The Numbers Apart

<u>Directions:</u> Ask the student to break apart the numbers into pairs.
Have the student show 2 ways to decompose each number. (Example: 5 = 2 + 3 and 5 = 4 + 1)
Record your work with a picture and/or an equation. You can use objects to help you.

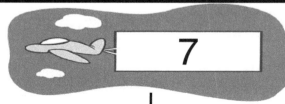

one way	another way

Possible Answers for 7 = 0+7, 1+6, 2+5, 3+4, 4+3, 5+2, 6+1, 7+0

Equation: 7 = ___ + ___	Equation: 7 = ___ + ___

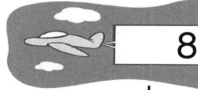

one way	another way

Possible Answers for 8 = 0+8, 1+7, 2+6, 3+5, 4+4, 5+3, 6+2, 7+1, 8+0

Equation: 8 = ___ + ___	Equation: 8 = ___ + ___

Standard: Math I Operations & Algebraic Thinking I K.OA.3   ©www.CoreCommonStandards.com

Level: Kindergarten   Name: _____

Breaking The Numbers Apart

<u>Directions:</u> Ask the student to break apart the numbers into pairs.
Have the student show 2 ways to decompose each number. (Example: 5 = 2 + 3 and 5 = 4 + 1)
Record your work with a picture and/or an equation. You can use objects to help you.

9

one way   ### another way

Possible Answers for 9 = 0+9, 1+8, 2+7, 3+6, 4+5, 5+4, 6+3, 7+2, 8+1, 9+0

Equation: 9 = ___ + ___   Equation: 9 = ___ + ___

10

one way   ### another way

Possible Answers for 10 = 0+10, 1+9, 8+2, 3+7, 6+4, 5+5, 6+4, 7+3, 8+2, 9+1, 10+0

Equation: 10 = ___ + ___   Equation: 10 = ___ + ___

Standard: Math I Operations & Algebraic Thinking I K.OA.3   ©www.CoreCommonStandards.com

Level: Kindergarten   Name: _____

Numbers That Make Ten

<u>Directions:</u> Draw a line from a number on the left to its partner on the right.
When you add the numbers together, they will make 10.

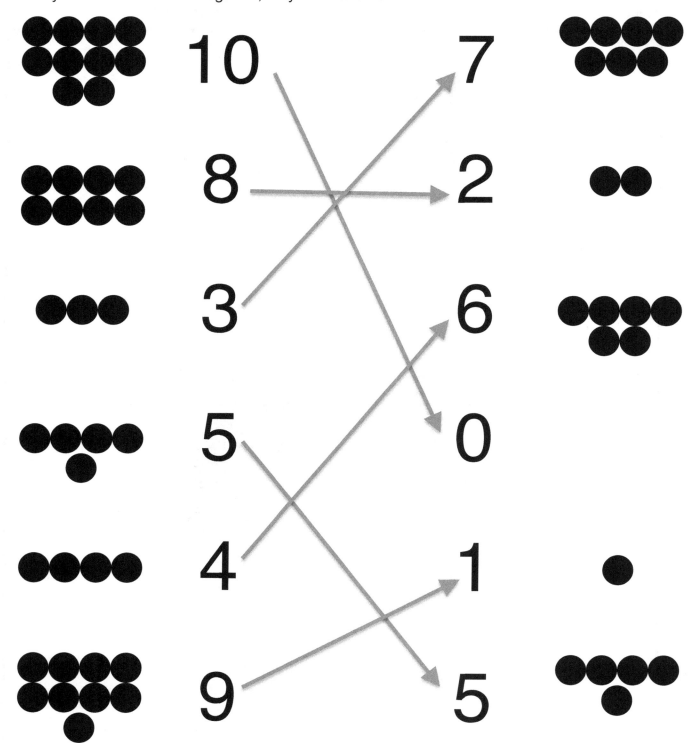

Standard: Math | Operations & Algebraic Thinking | K.OA.4   ©www.CoreCommonStandards.com

Name: _____

Find The Number That Makes 10

Directions: Find the number that makes 10 when added to the given number. You may draw a picture to show your thinking.

$5 + \underline{}5 = 10$	$6 + \underline{}4 = 10$
$7 + \underline{}3 = 10$	$2 + \underline{}8 = 10$
$4 + \underline{}6 = 10$	$3 + \underline{}7 = 10$
$8 + \underline{}2 = 10$	$1 + \underline{}9 = 10$

Standard: Math I Operations & Algebraic Thinking I K.OA.4   ©www.CoreCommonStandards.com

Name: _____

Addition Facts To 5

Time: _____

Correct: _____ / 10

Directions: Answer the addition facts below and record the time it took to complete.

$2 + 3 =$	5
$1 + 0 =$	1
$2 + 2 =$	4
$0 + 3 =$	3
$2 + 0 =$	2
$0 + 5 =$	5
$3 + 2 =$	5
$4 + 0 =$	4
$1 + 2 =$	3
$0 + 1 =$	1

Name: _____

Addition Facts To 5

Time: _____
Correct: _____ / 10

Directions: Answer the addition facts below and record the time it took to complete.

$1 + 1 =$ 1

$5 + 0 =$ 5

$3 + 0 =$ 3

$2 + 1 =$ 3

$0 + 4 =$ 4

$1 + 4 =$ 5

$3 + 1 =$ 4

$1 + 3 =$ 4

$0 + 2 =$ 2

$4 + 1 =$ 5

Name: _____

Subtraction Facts To 5

Time: _____
Correct: _____ / 10

<u>Directions:</u> Answer the subtraction facts below and record the time it took to complete.

3 - 1 =	2
2 - 0 =	0
2 - 2 =	0
5 - 4 =	1
3 - 3 =	0
1 - 0 =	1
4 - 3 =	1
4 - 4 =	0
5 - 1 =	4
4 - 0 =	4

Name: _____

Subtraction Facts To 5

Time: _____

Correct: _____ / 10

Directions: Answer the subtraction facts below and record the time it took to complete.

5 - 2 = 3

3 - 0 = 3

2 - 1 = 1

1 - 1 = 0

5 - 3 = 2

4 - 1 = 3

5 - 0 = 5

5 - 5 = 0

4 - 2 = 2

3 - 2 = 1

Name: _____

Counting Tens and Ones

<u>Directions:</u> Count the tens and ones and write the number each group makes.

1.

tens	ones
2	0

20

2.

tens	ones
2	1

21

3.

tens	ones
1	7

17

4.

tens	ones
1	5

15

5.

tens	ones
2	2

22

6.

tens	ones
1	3

13

7.

tens	ones
1	4

14

8.

tens	ones
1	6

16

9.

tens	ones
1	2

12

10.

tens	ones
1	8

18

11.

tens	ones
1	9

19

12.

tens	ones
1	1

11

Standard: Math I Operations & Algebraic Thinking I K.NBT.1   ©www.CoreCommonStandards.com

Name: _____

Drawing Tens and Ones

Directions: Look at the number in each box. Draw tens and ones to represent the number. You can use objects to help you. Try to write an equation for each number.

<u>18</u> 10 + 8 = 18	<u>17</u> 10 + 7 = 17 draw picture
<u>19</u> 10 + 9 = 19 draw picture	<u>16</u> 10 + 6 = 16 draw picture
<u>10</u> 10 + 0 = 10 draw picture	<u>13</u> 10 + 3 = 13 draw picture
<u>11</u> 10 + 1 = 11 draw picture	<u>14</u> 10 + 4 = 14 draw picture

Name: _____

Measure Words

<u>Directions:</u> Show student the pictures below. Ask student to use words such as **big, little, long, short, heavy**, and **light** to describe the pictures below.
(Teachers can record answers for student if needed.)

The mouse is	The pyramids
short, little, or light	are
	tall, heavy, big

The snake is	The feathers
long	are
	light

The elephant	The worm is
is	
heavy, big	little, light

The child is	The cupcake
	is
short, little, light	little, light

Standard: Math I Measurement & Data I K.MD.1   ©www.CoreCommonStandards.com

Name: _____

Measuring Up

Directions: Choose a word from the box to describe the pictures below.

heavy	light	tall	short	big	little

light or small

tall, big

big, heavy

short, little

heavy

little, short

little

short

tall, big

Standard: Math I Measurement & Data I K.MD.1

©www.CoreCommonStandards.com

Name: _answers vary_____

Comparing Measurements

<u>Directions:</u> Ask student to compare two objects and describe the difference between the two using words like **bigger, smaller, taller, shorter, thicker, thinner, heavier,** and **lighter.** Teachers can record for the student.

Sample answers are:
Rackets = smaller, shorter, bigger, taller, thicker, thinner

Apples = bigger, smaller, heavier, lighter

Trees = smaller, shorter, bigger, taller

Packages = thinner, thicker, heavier, lighter, smaller, bigger

Anchor & Balloon = heavier, lighter

Building & Blocks = heavier, lighter, bigger, smaller

Standard: Math I Measurement & Data I K.MD.2   ©www.CoreCommonStandards.com

Level: Kindergarten   Name: _____

Comparing Sizes

Directions: Look at the two pictures in each square. Circle the word that best describes the picture the arrow is pointing to. Your teacher can read the words to you if you need help.

Name: _____

Sorting Shapes

<u>Directions:</u> Look at the shapes below. Color the triangles blue, the squares red, and the circles green. Count the shapes and write their amounts on page 2.

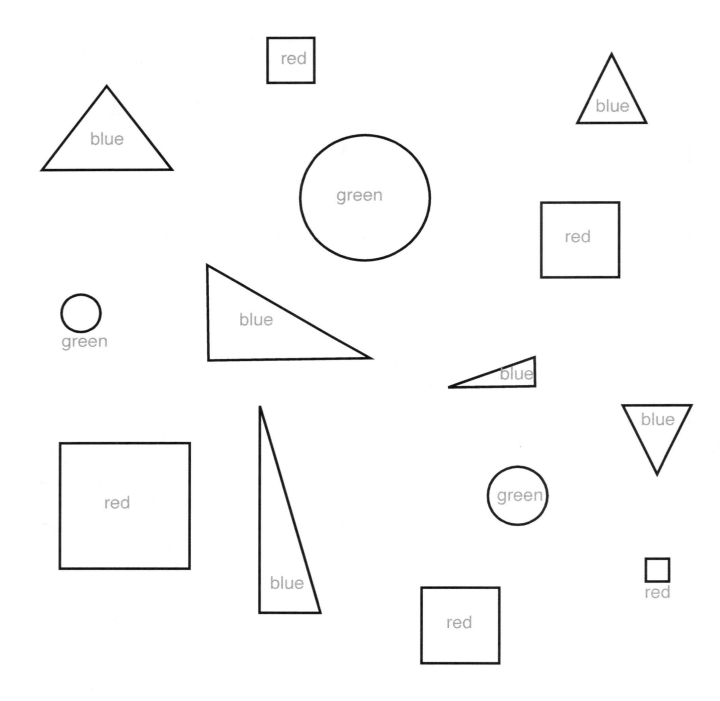

Name: _____

How Many?

☐ squares	◯ circles	△ triangles
5	3	6

Write the above numbers in order.

first	second	third
3	5	6

Standard: Math I Measurement & Data I K.MD.3

Classify, Count, and Sort

<u>Directions:</u> Circle the pictures on the right to match the categories below. Then, count how many are in each category and answer the questions below.

CATEGORY	CIRCLE COLOR	HOW MANY ARE THERE?
Numbers	RED	6
Consonants	GREEN	4
Vowels	BLUE	2

Which Category has the most items?

(Numbers)   (Consonants)   (Vowels)

Which Category has the least items?

(Numbers)   (Consonants)   (Vowels)

Arrange the Categories from least to greatest:

VOWELS	CONSONANTS	NUMBERS

Least ⟶ Most

Level: Kindergarten   Name: _____

Classify, Count, and Sort

Directions: Circle the pictures on the right to match the categories below. Then, count how many are in each category and answer the questions below.

CATEGORY	CIRCLE COLOR	HOW MANY ARE THERE?
Blue Mouse	BLUE	8
Red Mouse	RED	4
Orange Mouse	ORANGE	5
Green Mouse	GREEN	3

Which Category has the most items?

(**Blue**)   (Red)   (Orange)   (Green)

Which Category has the least items?

(Blue)   (Red)   (Orange)   (**Green**)

Arrange the Categories from least to greatest:

GREEN	RED	ORANGE	BLUE

Least ⟶ Most

Standard: Math I Measurement & Data I K.MD.3   ©www.CoreCommonStandards.com

Level: Kindergarten   Name: _____

Classify, Count, and Sort

<u>Directions:</u> Circle the pictures on the right to match the categories below. Then, count how many are in each category and answer the questions below.

CATEGORY	CIRCLE COLOR	HOW MANY ARE THERE?
Animals	RED	7
Fruits	GREEN	5
People	BLUE	4

Which Category has the most items?

(**Animals**)   (Fruits)   (People)

Which Category has the least items?

(Animals)   (Fruits)   (**People**)

Arrange the Categories from least to greatest:

(PEOPLE)   (FRUITS)   (ANIMALS)

Least ——————————————➤ Most

Name: _____

Classify, Count, and Sort

<u>Directions:</u> Circle the pictures on the right to match the categories below. Then, count how many are in each category and answer the questions below.

CATEGORY	CIRCLE COLOR	HOW MANY ARE THERE?
Meats	RED	2
Vegetables	GREEN	4
Dairy	BLUE	3
Fruits	PURPLE	7

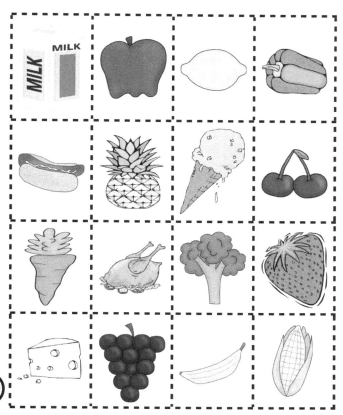

Which Category has the most items?

(Meats) (Vegetables) (Dairy) (**Fruits**)

Which Category has the least items?

(**Meats**) (Vegetables) (Dairy) (Fruits)

Arrange the Categories from least to greatest:

MEATS	DAIRY	VEGETABLES	FRUITS

Least ————————————————————▶ Most

Name: _____

What's the Position?

Directions: Choose a word from the box to describe where the ball is located.

above	below	beside	in front of	behind	next to

above	in front of	beside, next to

below	next to, beside	behind

Standard: Math I Geometry I K.G.1

©www.CoreCommonStandards.com

Name: _____

Draw the Position

Directions: Look at the farm picture. Draw the objects where the positional words say to.

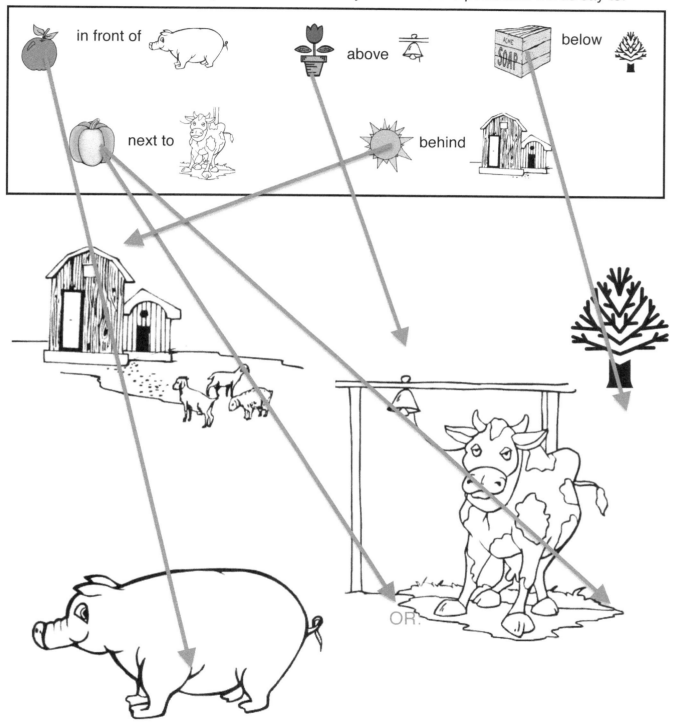

Level: Kindergarten   Name: _____

What Shape is It?

Directions:

Color all the triangles blue.

Color all the squares red.

Color all the rectangles orange.

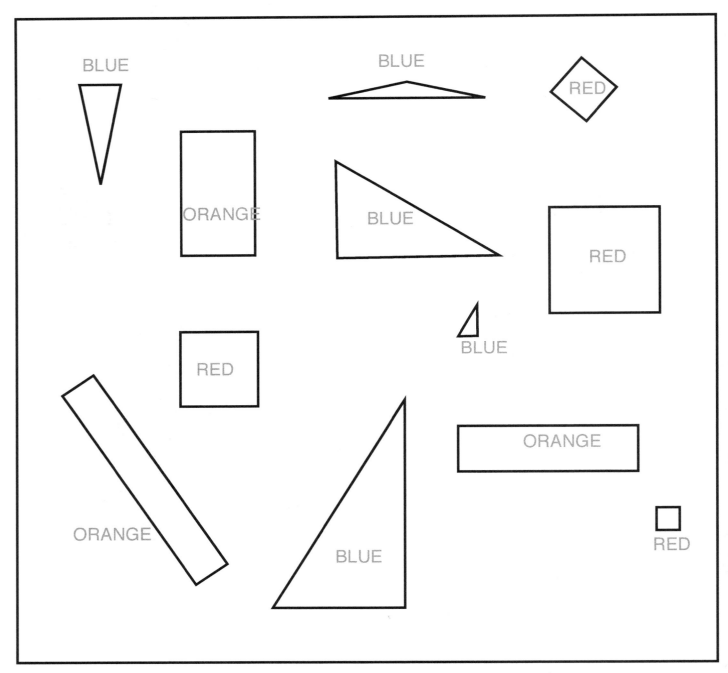

Standard: Math I Geometry I K.G.2   ©www.CoreCommonStandards.com

Level: Kindergarten   Name: _____

What Shape is It?

Directions:

Color all the circles green.

Color all the hexagons yellow.

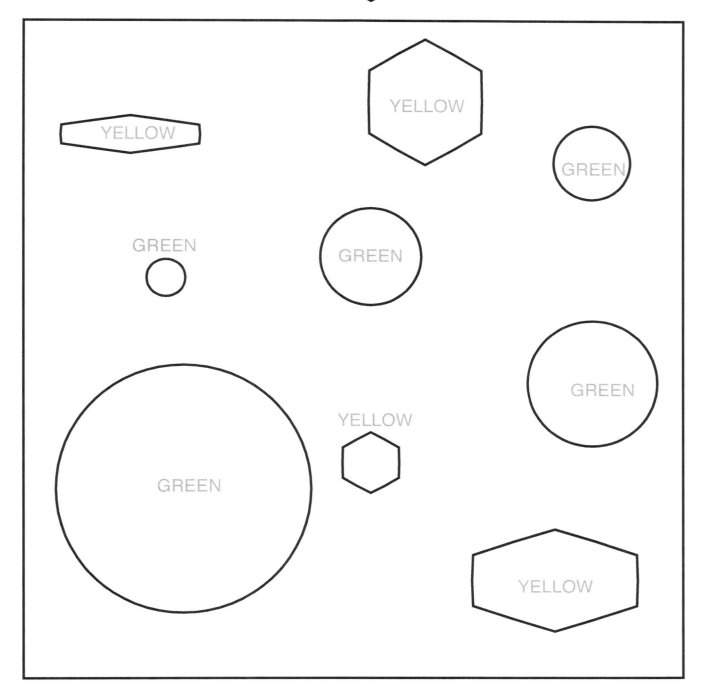

Standard: Math I Geometry I K.G.2   ©www.CoreCommonStandards.com

Level: Kindergarten   Name: _____

Two-D or Three-D?

<u>Directions:</u> Look at the pictures below. Are they 2-dimensional (flat) or 3-dimensional (solid)? Write 2-D or 3-D under the correct pictures.

3D	2D	3D
3D	3D	2D
2D	3D	2D

Name: _____

3-D Shapes

Directions: Draw a line to match the picture to its 3-dimensional or 2-dimensional shape name.

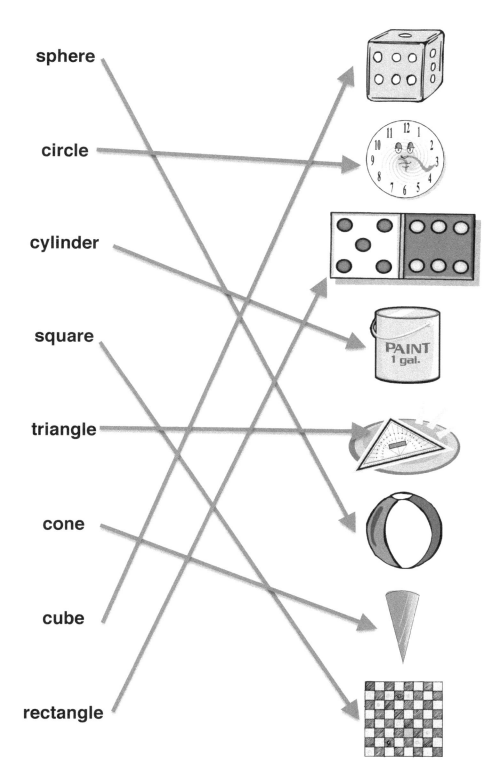

sphere

circle

cylinder

square

triangle

cone

cube

rectangle

Level: Kindergarten

Name: _____

Comparing 2-D and 3-D Shapes

Directions: Compare the two-dimensional and three-dimensional shapes below. Tell how many sides and vertices/corners each shape has. Then, tell how these shapes are the same and how they are different. What else do you notice about these shapes?

Two-Dimensional Shapes	Three-Dimensional Shapes	Same	Different
____ sides ____ corners	____ sides ____ corners		SQUARE VS. CUBE square = 4 sides and 4 corners cube = 6 faces made of 12 sides (edges) and 8 corners (vertices). same = both have square shapes included different = one has corners, the other has vertices, and being 3D adds many more sides and corners.
____ sides ____ corners	____ sides ____ corners	TRIANGLE VS. SQUARE PYRAMID triangle = 3 sides and 3 corners pyramid = 5 faces made of 8 sides (edges) and 5 corners (vertices). same = have triangles different = one has corners, the other has vertices, and being 3D adds many more sides and corners.	

Standard: Math | Geometry | K.G.4

©www.CoreCommonStandards.com

Level: Kindergarten   Name: _____

Comparing 2-D and 3-D Shapes

Directions: Compare the two-dimensional and three-dimensional shapes below. Cut out the shapes.
Look at the sides and angles of each 2-D and 3-D shape.
Use the charts on pages 2 and 3 to sort the shapes different ways. Explain your thinking.

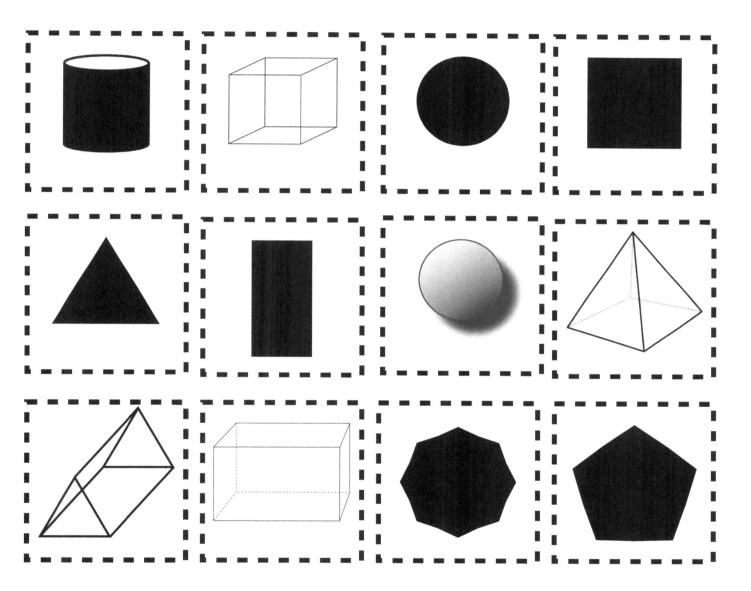

Standard: Math | Geometry | K.G.4   ©www.CoreCommonStandards.com

Name: ______________________________

Comparing 2-D and 3-D Shapes

Directions: Use the charts below to sort the shapes different ways. Explain your thinking.

No Sides or Angles	Only One Face	Has Triangles
circle sphere cylinder	circle square triangle rectangle octagon pentagon	triangle pyramid triangular prism

Standard: Math | Geometry | K.G.4

Has Squares	More Than Three Sides	3-Dimensional
cube square square pyramid rectangular prism	cube square rectangle pyramid triangular prism rectangular prism octagon pentagon	cube cylinder sphere pyramid triangular prism rectangular prism

Name: _____

Making Shapes

Directions: Look around you. What shapes do you see? Using clay balls and toothpicks, construct different 2-dimensional and 3-dimensional shapes that you see around you. Describe the shapes to a partner. Draw and label your shapes below.

answers vary

What are some things you learned about shapes?

_____

_____

_____

Standard: Math I Geometry I K.G.5

Name: _____

Making Shapes

Directions: Using clay balls and toothpicks, construct the shapes below. Then, count the sides (lines), vertices (corners), and faces (flat parts). Write the data into the chart.

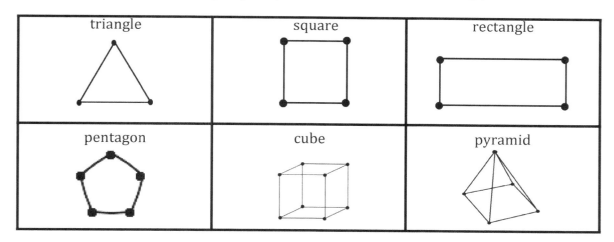

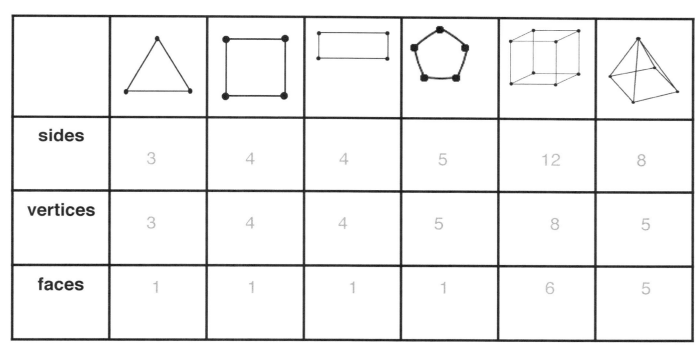

	 ▲	 ■	 ▭	 ⬠	 ◻	 ◭
sides	3	4	4	5	12	8
vertices	3	4	4	5	8	5
faces	1	1	1	1	6	5

How is a square different from a cube? Explain.

A square is flat or 2D, while a cube is 3D. Cubes have more vertices and sides.

_____

_____

_____

Standard: Math I Geometry I K.G.5   ©www.CoreCommonStandards.com

Name: _____

Making More Shapes

Directions: Use pattern or attribute blocks, or other shapes to create new shapes. Connect triangles, squares, rectangles, rhombuses, and other 2-D shapes to make larger shapes. What shapes did you use to make a new shape? Draw and label your shapes below.

answers vary

Name: _____

Making More Shapes

Directions: Using skinny straws and twist ties, construct 2-D shapes. Connect 2-D shapes to make new 2-D shapes and 3-D shapes. Draw some of the shapes you created. Label the shapes.

answers vary

What 2-D shapes do you see in some of the 3-D shapes you created?

_____

_____

_____

©www.CoreCommonStandards.com

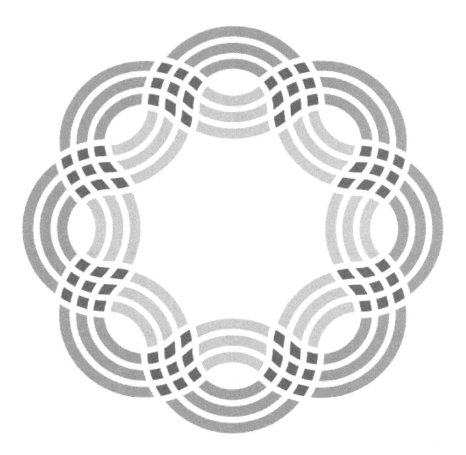

CPSIA information can be obtained
at www.ICGtesting.com
Printed in the USA
BVHW011722220620
582086BV00005B/88

9 781508 645757